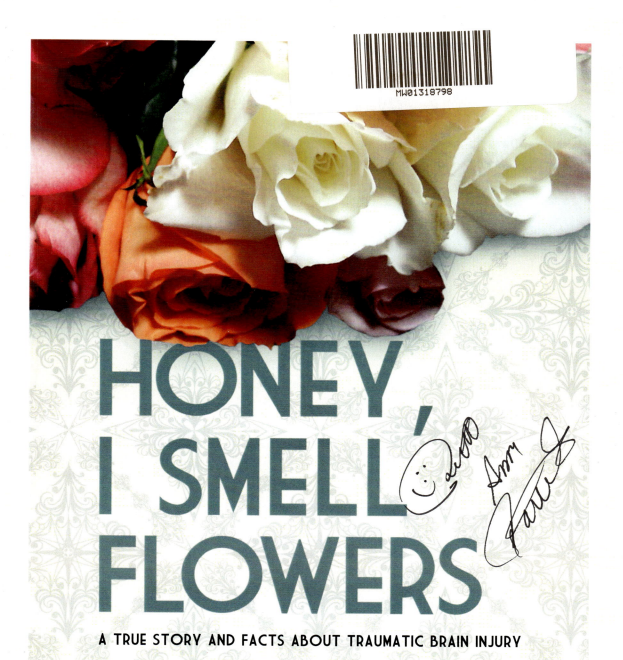

HONEY, I SMELL FLOWERS

A TRUE STORY AND FACTS ABOUT TRAUMATIC BRAIN INJURY

BY RUTH ANN BARTELS

Dedication

I dedicate this book to Michelle who fought the fight and kept on fighting to get her life back. She was and is a warrior.

Acknowledgments

Thanks to family and friends who cried with us and prayed with us and helped us in countless ways during Michelle's recovery.

Special thanks to my husband who was a pillar of strength throughout this ordeal and then encouraged me to write this book.

Thanks also to Bryan Health and Madonna Rehabilitation Hospital for teaching all of us how to emerge on the other side.

Mega Kudos to Sandy for using her talents and artistry to edit out the hospital and rehab backgrounds that were in the originial photos of Michelle's flowers. You made this book "blossom."

About the author

Ruth Ann is a wife and mother and was a medical technologist throughout her professional career. She served as Director of Professional Services for a large Regional Reference Laboratory in Omaha, Nebraska. Her daughter, Michelle, suffered a Traumatic Brain Injury in 2008. Ruth Ann has written the book she wishes someone had given her while she sat with Michelle in ICU and through Rehab therapies. It is a story of Michelle's fight to recover and includes pertinent information for others that are confronting the complications that come with injury to the brain.

Copyright © 2014 by Ruth Ann Bartels
Printed in the United States of America.

All rights reserved. No part of this book may be reproduced, stored in a retrieval system, or transmitted in any form or by any means, electronic, mechanical, photocopying, recording, or otherwise, except for brief reviews, without the prior written permission of Ruth Ann Bartels. www.bookabouttbi.com.

TABLE OF CONTENTS

Introduction v

Chapter 1: Monday, February 11, 2008 1
    California Here We Come

Chapter 2: Tuesday, February 12, 2008 15
    What is this "TBI" Thing?

Chapter 3: Wednesday, February 13, 2008 19
    "Mom, Check on Aidan!"

Chapter 4: Thursday, February 14, 2008 27
    Valentine's Day

Chapter 5: Friday, February 15, 2008 31
    Watch Out For The Tricycles!

Chapter 6: Saturday, February 16, 2008 35
    "I Would Never Make a Roast!"

Chapter 7: Sunday, February 17, 2008 39
    "We Have Witnessed The Strength That Comes From YOU When Hundreds Are Joined In Prayer!"

Chapter 8: Monday, February 18, 2008 43
    A Bedside Manicure and Pedicure

Chapter 9: Tuesday, February 19, 2008 47
    Let's Make Cookies!

Chapter 10: Wednesday, February 20, 2008 51
    A 3:00 AM Wake-Up Call

Chapter 11: Thursday, February 21, 2008 53
    Grace's Lunch Money Windfall

Chapter 12: Friday, February 22, 2008 59
    "Let's Go, Mom!"

Chapter 13: Saturday, February 23, 2008 63
    Alice . . .Betty . . .Carol

Chapter 14: Sunday, February 24, 2008 65
    More "Phantom" Actions

Chapter 15: Monday, February 25, 2008 67
    "Mom, I Have Always Needed You!"

Chapter 16: Tuesday, February 26, 2008 71
    Mom and Michelle Draw Up a Contract

Chapter 17: Wednesday, February 27, 2008 77
   "I'll have 1/2 lb Summer Sausage Cut In 1/8 Inch Thick Slices."

Chapter 18: Thursday, February 28, 2008..81
   "Mom, I'm So Glad You're Back!"

Chapter 19: Friday, February 29, 2008 87
   The Fog is Lifting

Chapter 20: Saturday and Sunday March 1&2, 2008 91
   Today Michelle Cried!

Chapter 21: Week 1 of Outpatient Therapy 93
   March 3-March 9, 2008
   "Mom, You Don't Know How Comforting It Is To Remember Yesterday."

Chapter 22: Week 2 of Outpatient Therapy 99
   March 10-March 16, 2008
   "Well, Mom, Did I Pass Brownies 101?"

Chapter 23: Week 3 of Outpatient Therapy 101
   March 17-March 23, 2008
   "It May Take 6-12 Months To Get My Stamina Back."

Chapter 24: Week 4 of Outpatient Therapy 105
   March 24-March 30, 2008
   Happy Easter, Everyone

Chapter 25: April, 2008...109
   Happy Birthday, Geran! Happy Birthday, Grace!

Chapter 26: The Remaining Months of 2008.....................................113
   Bible School, Mayo Clinic, Family Reunions

Chapter 27: Michelle's Chapter 119

Chapter 28: Six Things I Wish I had Known 121
   One Thing I'm Glad I Knew

Appendix..127

Glossary 128

Glasgow Coma Scale 130

Ranchos Los Amigos Scale...131

Finding The Right Rehabilitation Center..137

Is This A Concussion?...140

A Chronology of Michelle's Medical Episodes 150

Bibliography 156

Honey, I Smell Flowers

Introduction

If you picked up this book because you thought it would be about flowers, I am sorry. There are some lovely pictures of flowers at the beginning of each chapter and I hope you will view them. They are pictures of flowers my daughter received while recovering from an automobile accident that resulted in a Traumatic Brain Injury or TBI, as everyone calls it. I took pictures of the flowers because I knew she wouldn't remember them and I wanted her to see the beautiful arrangements people had sent along with the words of encouragement they conveyed in their cards.

I hope you'll decide to read the book. Everyone should know the facts about TBI's and how serious they are medically, emotionally, and financially. They strike without warning and change lives in an instant. There were so many things I didn't know about TBI's. I wanted to write the book that I wish someone had given me while I was sitting in Michelle's room watching her struggle to return to her wonderful life.

If you are sitting in an intensive care unit with a loved one and someone hands you this book, go to Chapter 28 and read "Things I wish I had known."

If you are into day 2 or 3 or 4 of recovery, read the chapter information under "My Narrative" where I explain what happened to Michelle each step along the way to her recovery.

Finally, I have included medical notes from the moment the call went to 911, through the ER Trauma Unit, intensive care, rehabilitation, and outpatient care.

I have included some of the medical notes with each chapter. I believe they will give you insight into the level and intensity of therapy necessary to bring about a positive recovery. I personally wanted to have the medical notes to validate my observations and journaling. I wanted to see the staff's interpretations of their interactions with Michelle compared to my daily journaling notes. I have all the medical notes and am willing to share them with anyone that would like a complete review of Michelle's daily therapies. My contact for these notes is found on page 155.

Some authors, and others working in the field of TBI's, consider concussions a mild TBI. Others think they are their own classification of brain injury. There is much overlapping between the two, but both deserve medical attention and medical monitoring before returning to normal activities.

Lastly, thank you for reading this book and I hope you will gain insight into the lives of the millions of people that struggle with brain injuries each and every year. A TBI affects not just the patient, but the patient's family. In our case it was not only us, as parents, but Michelle's husband and their 4 little kids and Michelle's sisters and their families. Lives are changed in an instant and everyone's world is different from that day forward.

God Bless you for using this book to learn more about the traumatic events that 1.7 million civilians and over 200,000 military personnel suffer each year. Please pause to say a silent prayer for the patients and their families as they struggle to adjust to life after TBI.

Chapter 1

Monday, February 11, 2008

California Here We Come

MY NARRATIVE

Larry and I left frigid Nebraska for a week's vacation in Palm Desert, CA. It was 3 degrees above zero when we boarded our flight and we could hardly wait to get to the California desert to feel the warmth of sun on our faces again. We had an early morning flight and since we were flying west and picking up hours along the way, it was still mid morning in California when we arrived.

The sun was shining brightly and the captain of the aircraft announced it was 60 degrees in LA as we were landing. As always when I fly, I lifted up a silent "Thank you" toward the heavens for our safe flight and we headed for the baggage terminal and our great adventure for the week ahead. The baggage terminal was our first clue that perhaps this was not going to be a normal week after all. My suitcase had not arrived and upon checking we discovered this was not unusual. I began to worry when the first place the clerk called was Newark, NJ to see if it had arrived there. After the clerks checked several other destinations and were unable to find my luggage, we decided to go get our rental car and let the airlines bring my luggage to the resort once they found it. We were anxious to begin our R&R.

We stepped out of the terminal building into the bright welcome warmth of sunshine and I said, "Honey, I smell flowers!" Something was already in bloom in southern California and it smelled wonderful! I turned on my cell phone and within a minute it rang.

It was a call that would forever change our lives. I have three daughters and it was my middle child calling. Melissa told me Michelle, my youngest, had been in a car accident and Michelle's twins had been with her. The twins were not hurt but Michelle was unconscious and Michelle's husband Greg had frantically called Melissa and told her to "find your parents!" Michelle and Greg had met that morning to sign papers to refinance their mortgage so Greg was following her and saw the accident as it happened. Greg called 911 and an ambulance was on the way. Melissa had no more information and said she would call me as soon as she got to BryanLGH West or as soon as she had more information from Greg.

By the time I finished the call, the bus to the rental car agency had arrived and Larry guided me on while I tried to collect my thoughts to tell him what had happened. Larry is a physical therapist and I am a medical technologist so medical emergencies usually do not cause us to go into "alarm" mode. We were relieved our 3 year old granddaughters had not been injured and just assumed Michelle had been knocked out from the impact. We decided to go ahead and pick up our car and drive to our resort and make decisions when we knew more.

I have no memory of our nearly 1 hour drive to the resort. When you are busy reminding God about Michelle's family—6 year old Grace, 4 year old Geran, and 3 year old twins, Aidan and Alysen—and explaining to him how much they needed her, you don't really notice your surroundings as you travel.

Just as we arrived at the resort, my cell phone rang. Again it was Melissa who had to relay the news to me that Michelle had been taken to the trauma center hospital in Lincoln and was scheduled for surgery to implant a probe in her brain to monitor the pressure inside her skull. She had not regained consciousness in the ambulance or in the emergency room and her husband had had to sign a release to remove part of her skull if the pressure was building inside her brain. We immediately knew we had to return home, this was not going to be a week of sun and fun!

The resort where we had planned to stay was very helpful and understanding when we went into the lobby to cancel our reservation. We asked if we could stay in the lobby and make some phone calls and try to arrange for our flights home and they actually gave us a suite to stay in for as long as it took to make our final reservations. Of course, having a sobbing woman standing in your lobby is probably not the best advertisement for a resort so finding us a place to recover was probably also in their best interest! However, I will always appreciate the comfort of that suite for the many phone calls, the bathroom, and Kleenex, and the small patio that again brought me the smell of fresh flowers while we waited.

When you have a traumatic shock, your mind flies randomly in many directions. Some of the thoughts flying through my brain are panic and fear and hopelessness. What would we do if Michelle died? How could we help Greg raise the kids? How could this have happened? Why can't we get home sooner? Other thoughts are very directed and logical. When can we get a flight? How can our airline tickets be used to get home? Once my luggage is found, I don't want it delivered to the Palm Desert resort, I need it at the airport when we leave or I need it in Nebraska. Can the people at the airport understand this?

Larry and I had purposely picked a small airlines on which to travel because they flew non-stop into LA's Ontario airport, which was near our destination. The flight had been wonderful but the down side was that they did not have many flights back to Omaha. In fact, they did not have a flight back until 6:00 PM that night. After trying many other options, it became obvious that returning with the airline we had flown on in the morning was still the best option for getting home—and hopefully recovering my luggage before we left California.

As we prepared to leave our safe little cocoon that the resort had provided, we heard from Melissa again. Michelle was in intensive care. She had a breathing tube and a probe in the brain but no physical injuries. She had been wearing a seat belt and the Yukon Denali she was driving had air bags which had deployed. She had been fortunate not to have any broken bones. Melissa had stayed with the twins in the emergency room as they were examined for any injuries. Aidan had a broken arm. It was the kind of break my husband calls "green stick" and it only needed a splint but she was hurting and both she and Alysen were pretty traumatized from the accident. Having just turned 3 the last day in January, they were able to state very clearly, "Mommy drove into a tree and she went to sleep and she couldn't wake up!"

Melissa's husband Jason left work and came to the hospital to help Melissa with the kids. He stayed with Geran while Melissa accompanied the twins for their examinations and the for Aidan's x-ray.

Greg's parents drove the 2 hours to Lincoln from Humphrey, NE and they were helping Melissa and Jason at the hospital with the four "Grands" (my special name for my Grandkids!). My oldest daughter Laura and her husband lived in Lawrence, KS and were on their way to Lincoln to help. Greg didn't leave Michelle's side and we were in California trying to get home.

When we arrived at the airport, the airlines told us they had found my luggage but they couldn't get it to Ontario in time to meet our plane so they were flying the luggage directly to Omaha and they PROMISED it would be at the Omaha terminal when we arrived. Knowing there would be no food on the plane, we decided to have dinner at the airport before our flight. During our dinner in the late afternoon in LA, my cell phone began to ring about every five minutes. The Lincoln television stations had made Michelle's accident the lead local news at 5 and 6 o'clock and my friends had begun to call. They told us that one of the station's lead-ins was, "Young Mother Fighting For Her Life." We later found out that was an "over-dramatization" of the accident but when you're 1500 miles away, that news was devastating to us. Most of the friends that were calling did not know we were out of town and were calling to see how they could help.

The last call I got before the battery died on my cell phone was from my boss in Omaha. He is a pathologist and knows the dangers of head injuries. I have worked with him for over 20 years and Michelle worked at our Omaha laboratory in client services and microbiology for several years. Someone from our Lincoln Lab had called him about the Lincoln television report. He offered his support to the family and told me to take as much time as I needed to help Michelle. It is hard to be strong when your boss is trying hard not to cry. Our dinner lost its appeal and we headed to our gate to await our departure.

Larry's cell phone still had power, so our last call to Melissa before we left confirmed that Laura and Dirk had made it to Lincoln, Greg's folks had taken "The Grands" to Greg and Michelle's house and were staying with them for the night, Melissa and Jason had been joined by some of Greg's friends and they took over one section of the ICU waiting area to keep up the hourly vigil. Greg was planning to stay the night and Melissa assured us that Michelle was stable and we should try to get some sleep once we got home.

We arrived in Omaha at 12:00 Midnight and a very sleepy-looking attendant was waiting at the Express Jet ticket counter along with my luggage! By the time we got our car and headed the 60 miles home to Lincoln the temperature was 12 below zero and we knew we would be lucky to lay our heads on our pillows by 1:30 A.M.

PERTINENT MEDICAL NOTES
LINCOLN FIRE AND RESCUE

RESPONSE INFORMATION:
  NATURE OF THE CALL: Traffic accident, 38-year-old female unconscious… Is breathing.
  LOCATION: 84th& Pioneers Blvd, Lincoln Nebraska.
  LOCATION TYPE: Street: street or driveway
  RESPONDED WITH: Multiple Lincoln fire and rescue units

PATIENT INFORMATION:
  NAME: S., Michelle
  DATE OF BIRTH: May 23, 1969 (38).
  SEX: Female.

INITIAL INFORMATION:
  PATIENT FOUND: Sitting upright in vehicle.
  CHIEF COMPLAINT: Primary – altered mental status
  PRESENT ILLNESS: Extent of injury unknown, Mechanism of injury unknown,
       cause of injury – motor vehicle versus fixed object.
  TRAUMA: Vehicular Injury Indicators – Dash Deformity
       Vehicular Injury Indicators -- High-Speed Impact
       Vehicular Injury Indicators – Steering Wheel Deformity,
       Vehicular Injury Indicators – Windshield Spider/Star
  RELEVANT PAST HISTORY: Patient's history is unknown
  MEDICATIONS: Unknown

ALLERGIES: Unknown

ASSESSMENTS:

BODY AREA	ASSESSMENT
Airway	Patient
Breathing	Agonal Respirations
Circulation	All Pulses Present
CNS	Other
Head	Assessed with No Abnormalities
Mental Status	Altered Level of Consciousness
Neck	Swelling and swelling over trachea

IMPRESSIONS:
  PRIMARY IMPRESSION: Trauma – closed head injury

VITAL SIGNS:

    Pulse   90 strong/regular
    Glasgow Coma Scale   E1 M1 V2 =4
    Respiratory   Agonal Rate 6 per minute

Notes: skin temperature: cool
- Skin color: normal colored
- Skin moisture: normal moisture
- Arm movement:
  - left absent
  - right absent
- Leg movement:
  - left absent
  - right absent
- Pupil reacts:
  - left – sluggish
  - right – sluggish
- Pupil dilation:
  - left – constricted
  - right – dilated
- Loss of Consciousness: unresponsive

TREATMENT SUMMARY

Treatment: Spinal Immobilization
Description
- Indication: Motor Vehicle Accident
- Initial MSC: MSC not intact
- Cervical collar: adult adjustable
- Method: extracted from car onto
- Secured on: long spine board
- CID: Sta-Blok
- Secured with: Spider Straps
- Result: Same MSC as initially
- Complications: none
- Procedure response: Unchanged
- Number of total attempts: One

Lincoln Fire and Rescue time line:

Received call:	11:21:03
Dispatched:	11:22:00
Enroute:	11:22:22
At Scene:	11:25:59
Transport:	11:54:20
Arrival at Emergency Room:	12:01
Hospital Admission:	12:24

BRYAN/LGH MEDICAL CENTER-WEST

TRIAGE:

ARRIVAL: Patient arrived by stretcher via ambulance from home. Accompanied by: EMT/paramedic. Patient entered the emergency room through the ambulance bay.
CHIEF COMPLAINT QUOTE\NOTE: Trauma 1MVC
DATE AND/OR TIME SYMPTOMS STARTED:
Approximately Monday, February 11, 2008 11:30
EMS PROCEDURES:
C – spine immobilization: C – spine immobilized with a hard c-collar with tape with head blocks and on a long spine board.
PAIN RELATED TO TODAY'S VISIT: Unable to obtain.
PAIN INDEX ASSESSMENT: Unable to rate pain level.

There are no obvious signs of distress.

DISPOSITION:

NURSING: Yes, this is a trauma patient, Trauma Category 1
ADMITTING DIAGNOSIS: TBI, seizure history
ADMISSION TYPE: Inpatient Trauma
ADMISSION AREA: ICU Telemetry
PATIENT ASSIGNED TO: 2 South bed W214
BED READY: Monday, February 11, 2008 12.25

NURSING NOTES:

12:00 PM: Monitoring: The patient is being monitored with automatic blood pressure cuff, cardiac monitor and O2 saturation monitor
- Temperature: 95.1
- Pulse: 72
- Blood pressure: 116/68
- Oxygen saturation: 100 %
- Respirations: patient intubated

12:01 PM: Medications were taken prior to arrival in the Emergency Department
Medications taken: Medications administered per EMS
- Lidocaine 60 mg IV
- Etomidate 18 mg IV
- Succinylcholine 90 mg IV
- Vercuronium 6 mg IV
- Versed 2 mg IV

EMERGENCY DEPARTMENT ORDERS FOR ADULT TRAUMA

NURSING:
1. Place on cardiac monitor.
2. Continuous pulse oximetry.
3. Complete neural assessment.
4. Immobilization: Hard Collar
5. Nasogastric tube: Insert
6. Foley catheter: Insert
7. Consultations: Anesthesiology

DIAGNOSTIC STUDIES: LAB

8. Category I: (type and cross match, Hemogram, BMP, TT, PTT, pregnancy test – serum, arterial blood gases, lactate level, urinalysis – routine, BAC, drugs of abuse screen, ionized calcium.)

RADIOLOGY:
Plain films: extremities both knees, both ankles.
CT scan: head without contrast
Cervical spine
Face
Chest
Hand

CARDIOLOGY:
ECG

MEDICATIONS:
IV: insert two number 14 or 16 gauge IV catheters
Attach 1000 mL Lactated Ringers to each IV and adjust rate according to patient need.
Tetanus booster if indicated. Give 250 units of human tetanus antitoxin if no previous immunization.
Morphine 5 mg IV every five minutes until pain rating is less than 5

TRAUMA SERVICE ADMISSION ORDER:

1. Admit to Trauma Service: ICU
2. Diagnosis: TBI
3. Condition: serious
4. Spine precautions: Hard Cervical Collar
5. Neurological Checks: Every Two Hours
6. Input and Outputs, Daily Weights.
7. Diet: NPO (nothing by mouth)
8. Activity: Bed rest
9. Elevate Head of Bed 30°
10. Respiratory therapy: Institute the Trauma Lung Volume Expansion Protocol, the Aerosolized Medication Protocol, and Oxygen Therapy Protocol.
11. Continuous Pulse Oximeter
12. Ventilator: maintain pressure control
13: Bowel Regimen
    Dulcolax suppository per rectum every day (may hold if more than 1 BM/day)
    Fleets enema as needed if no stool greater than two days
    Soapsuds enema if no BM after second Dulcolax suppository.
14. Tubes and Drains: Foley to Urometer. Insert Foley if no urine output in 6 hours.
15. Wound Care: Bacitracin/Neomycin/Polymyxin (Neosporin) ointment to abrasions
16 Glycemic control: Institute glycemic management – hyperglycemia and hypoglycemia adult
17. Deep Vein Thrombosis prophylaxis: SCD's thigh high, while in bed until independently ambulating
18. Diagnostic studies: Free Dilantin level every hour X3 Hemogram
    CMP and amylase in a.m. with ionized calcium, magnesium, phosphorus and lactate
    Chest X-ray in a.m. due to respiratory failure
    CT head in a.m. Reason: Follow-up TBI
    EEG now
19. IV fluids: (Traumatic Brain Injury) Normal Saline with Potassium Chloride 20 mEq at 50 mls/hour
20. Medications
    Famotidine (Pepcid) 20 mg IV
    Promethazine (Phenergan) 12.5 mg IV every 4 hours as needed
21. Please courtesy notify primary care physician of admission
22. Please contact physician on-call for consultation: Neurosurgery, Neurology
23. Nutritional services consultation.
24. Intervention nurse to evaluate if blood-alcohol level positive or positive drug screen.
25. Physiatry consult submission Glasgow Coma Scale was 8 or less.
26. Social services to consult within 24 hours for patient and family evaluation/orientation.
27. Physical therapy to evaluate and treat on first post trauma day
28. Occupational therapy to evaluate and treat on second post trauma day.
29. Evaluation on second post trauma day for rehabilitation potential.
30. Consult trauma director.
31. Call trauma team leader for: temperature greater than 100.5, heart rate greater than 120 or less than 50, SEP less than 90, or greater than 30, SpO2 less than 90%, urine output less than 30 mL/hour or less than 120 mL per 4 hours/, chest tube drainage greater than 200 mL per hour or for uncontrolled pain.
32. Ensure patient is admitted to trauma service.

TRAUMA ADULT CONTINUOUS ENTERAL FEEDING ORDER

Formulas: Impact with Fiber (immune enhancing, intact protein with fiber)
Rate: Initiate at 20 mL per hour now and increased by 20 mL every eight hours based on patient tolerance to goal rate. 80 mL
Residuals: Measure gastric residuals every 4 hours.
Diagnostic settings: Prealbumin level every Monday and Thursday while on tube feeding.
Standing orders: Elevate patient's head a minimum of 30°. Change pump set every 24 hours.

GLYCEMIC MANAGEMENT – HYPERGLYCEMIA AND HYPOGLYCEMIA:

Diagnostic Studies: Capillary Glucose Monitoring every 4 hours

PATIENT CONTROLLED ANALGESIA/CONTINUOUS INFUSION

Medications: Fentanyl 25 MCG/ML
Pulse oximetry: Continuous pulse oximetry, throughout PCA (patient controlled analgesia) use.

BREAKTHROUGH PAIN MANAGEMENT:

Call
Nausea: Prochlorperazine (Compazine) 5-10 mg PO/IV q 4-6 H PRN.
Pruritus (itching): Diphenhydramine (Benadryl) 25 mg PO/IV q 4 H PRN.

PASTORAL CARE:

I was with family down in ER from noon to 4 PM and continue to follow.
Feel free to page me as/if needed. Hospital chaplain

NEUROSURGEON CONSULTATION REPORT:

The patient is approximately mid-30-year-old female who was in a car in front of her husband. Her husband noted her head to be lolling back after coming off of a stop sign. She then crashed with her twin children in the back. The twins are doing quite well. Reportedly, at the scene, the patient had agonal respirations. Was given Vecuronium and intubated. Brought to the Bryan LGH Medical Center West Trauma Center.

CT scan reveals multiple contusions throughout her brain. No significant shift. She is under the effects of the medication. Her pupils are 4 and reactive. Given the patient's reported state prior to the Vecuronium being given as well as the multiple contusions seen on the CT, I elected to place an intraparenchymal monitoring device, which was placed in the right frontal region without difficulty. The initial pressure reading was 18. We will give her Fosphenytoin and follow while she is here. Of note, the patient reported seizure disorder that had not yet been worked up, although was going to be in the process of working it up. Eventually, she will need an MRI scan of her brain as well as a neurology consult and likely electroencephalogram.

NEUROLOGIST CONSULTATION REPORT: REASON FOR CONSULTATION:

Question of seizure prior to motor vehicle accident.

HISTORY OF PRESENT ILLNESS:

The patient is a middle-aged, white female who has a history of questionable syncopal episodes dating back to six years, evaluated by physicians in Lincoln as well as in Omaha. Not thought to be seizures apparently. Was on seizure medications only briefly. Apparently, had a motor vehicle accident today with a head injury with blood in the ventricle. There was some question of whether or not she had seizure prior to the accident. Husband was driving beside her at the time of the accident and notice kind of stiffening of the body. Also noted this after he came upon the accident. No seizure activity witnessed here. She was loaded with Dilantin.

PAST MEDICAL HISTORY:

Other than these three or four episodes of loss of consciousness in the past six years, otherwise unremarkable.

FAMILY HISTORY: Otherwise unremarkable.

SOCIAL HISTORY: Otherwise unremarkable.

REVIEW OF SYMPTOMS: Otherwise unremarkable.

NEUROLOGICAL EXAMINATION:

The patient is sedated with Fentanyl. She does kind of barely open her eyes. According to the nurse, she was following commands and squeezing a hand. She does not do that for me today. She has bilateral up going toes. Brisk reflexes throughout. Sensory examination not obtainable. Pupils 3 mm bilaterally. Eye movements are full.

IMPRESSION:

1. Closed head injury.
2. Possible seizure as cause of the initial accident.

PLAN/RECOMMENDATIONS:

Agree with Fosphenytoin. We will do an EEG but will wait until she is off Fentanyl, hopefully. We will get some records from Omaha to review.

RADIOLOGY:

CT spine cervical with contrast: negative CT scan cervical spine.
Impression: Negative CT scan cervical spine.

CT head without contrast
Clinical History. Multiple injuries

Findings: Axial noncontract images were obtained through the brain. The examination shows evidence of fluid within the paranasal sinuses potentially posttraumatic in nature. Evidence of a discrete skull fracture is not observed.

There is evidence of abnormality within the brain. There is evidence of intraventricular blood. Some of this is observed in the temporal horn while collections are also seen in the occipital and right lateral ventricle. Minimal blood is present in the third ventricle. Significant ventricular dilation is not seen.

Question a small amount of blood in the parenchyma posteromedial temporal lobe. Small petechial-type hemorrhages are also seen more superiorly in the right frontoparietal distribution, primarily centered in the white matter. The gray – white matter interfaces appear to be satisfactory at this point.

Impression: Post traumatic changes in the brain with blood in the ventricular system. Small amount of blood also observed in the parenchyma in the posteromedial temporal region and parietal/frontal distribution on the right. Small amount of blood may be present in the right basal ganglia but may be more apparent than real due to artifact. Extraaxial spaces intact.

Blood in the sinuses.

CT scan: Thoracic spine without contrast
Clinical History: Multiple Injuries.
Impression: Chronic changes lower thoracic distribution. Evidence of an acute compression deformity or other acute posttraumatic fracture is not seen. Mild degenerative changes seen in the mid thoracic distribution.

CT sinus\facial without contrast
Clinical History: Motor Vehicle Collision.
Impression: Changes to support sinusitis. Some blood may also be present. Evidence of an acute facial bone fracture not confirmed at this time. Mandible appears to be intact. Orbital and periorbital distributions in tact.

CT chest\abdomen like back/pelvis with contrast
Clinical History: Motor Vehicle Collision, Multiple Injuries
Impression: Negative CT scan of the chest, abdomen, and pelvis for any focal acute findings. No gross deformities to support fracture. No evidence of contusion or pneumothorax.

Knee routine three views
Clinical History: Multiple injuries.
Impression: Negative three-view right knee and three-view left knee

Ankle routine three views
Clinical History: Multiple injuries
Impression: Negative three-view left ankle and three-view right ankle.

MEDICATIONS 02/11/08

Magnesium Hydroxide Suspension 30 ML
Methylcellulose Tab 2000 MG
Nimodipine Cap 60 MG
Sennosides-Docusate Sodium Tab. Two tabs daily
Famotidine Injection 20 mg
Fosphenytoin Sodium Injection 100 PE
Sodium chloride 0.9% – 10 ML to flush lines
Bisacodyl Suppository 10 mg
Insulin sliding scale Novolog/Humalog
Chlorhexidine Gluconate Solution 15 ML for oral Care in mouth
Glucagon injection 1 mg
Lidocaine HCL Inj local anesthesia
Prochlorperazine Edisylate injection 5 mg and 10 mg IV push
Promethazine HCL inj 25 mg/ml IV push
Dextrose 50% IV push slowly over 5 to 10 minutes per hypoglycemia protocol
Albuterol Sulfate Solution 0.083%
Cefazolin Solution 1 g IV
DiphenhydrAMINE HCL inj 50 mg/ml IV push for pruritius (itching)
Naloxone HCL Inj 0.4 mg/mL
Acetaminophen Elixir 650 mg/20.3 ml if needed
Glucose chew tab 15 g three tabs if hypoglycemia symptoms worsen
Diphenhydramine HCL Cap 25 mg
Famotidine Tab 20 mg
Prochlorperazine Maleate Tab 10 mg PRN nausea
Prochlorperazine Maleate TAb 5 mg PRN nausea
Acetaminophen Suppository 650 mg
Lidocaine-Transparent Dressing Kit
Neomycin/Bacitracin/Polymyxin Ointment 30 GM tube top to Abrasions
Sodium chloride 0.9% 1000 ml
Sodium chloride 0.9% 500 ml
Fentanyl PCA 0.75 mg High Alert Med--2 person double check
Magnesium Sulfate 2 gm Infuse over 2 hours
Magnesium Sulfate 4 gm Infuse over 4 hours
Calcium chloride 13.8 M EQ infuse over 30 minute protocol
Calcium chloride 27.2 M EQ infuse over 60 minute protocol
Calcium chloride 40.8 M EQ infuse over 60 minute protocol
Potassium phosphate 15 MMole infuse over two hours per protocol
Potassium phosphate 30 MMole infuse over four hours per protocol
Potassium phosphate 45 MMole infuse over six hours per protocol
Sodium phosphate 15 MMole infuse over two hours per protocol
Sodium phosphate 30 MMole infuse over four hours per protocol
Sodium phosphate 45 MMole infuse over six hours per protocol

CARE NOTE SUPPLEMENT

02/11/08 13:00 Initially unresponsive due to neural muscular blocks. Pupils: right sluggish, left brisk. Continue to monitor.

02/11/08 15:20 Assessed and attempted to reorient. Opens eyes, agitated, grasps but questions command. Moves all extremities. Continue assess and reorient.

02/11/08 19:40 Assessment completed patient on ventilator tube. ICP bolt in place. ICP <10, Patient opens eyes to verbal stimuli. Follows commands with four extremities. Patient becomes agitated with calls, gags on vent frequently. Fentanyl infusing. Will continue to monitor.

02/11/08 21:30 PM: Elevated temperature. Dr. notified regarding elevated temperature patient given 650 mg Tylenol suppository, covered with blanket and wrapped.

02/12/08 02:05 AM Patient sat up in bed, ICP catheter dislodged, pulls out. Bolt remains in place. Dr. called and notified. Neural assessment completed. Bolt wrapped in betadine soaked gauze per doctor's orders. Will continue to monitor neuro status.

Chapter 2

Tuesday, February 12, 2008

What Is This "TBI" Thing?

MY NARRATIVE

    A few hours of sleep was all that was needed to regain energy and let the adrenaline take over. We were at the hospital by 7:00 AM. Greg said Michelle slept restlessly during the night, I don't think he got much sleep at all. She does have a bad cut on her right ankle and a bruise and abrasion on her left knee. She still has the breathing tube but the brain probe came out of her head when she sat up quickly during the night and since the pressure in her brain had been normal, they decided not to re-insert it. I was glad I did not have to see her with the probe sticking out of her head. We talked to her but she never opened her eyes so we didn't know if she knew we were there.

    Her first Physical Therapy treatment came at 9:00 AM, less than 24 hours after her accident. It is very important to have an early evaluation of strength of motion and cognition or understanding commands. Treatment plans for rehabilitation are begun immediately and the starting point for her further treatments is being planned based on these early results.

While we talked to her gently and lovingly, the therapist shook her shoulder firmly and insisted that she follow commands such as "lift up this arm" or "hold your arm stiff, don't let me bend it." To our surprise and delight, she could do each thing they asked with both arms and both legs. She never opened her eyes and they had to repeatedly shake her shoulder but she eventually followed each command and showed good control and strength. I knew that was a good thing. When the therapist finished, my husband smiled at me and gave me the "physical therapist's thumbs up" sign.

Friends and more relatives were beginning to gather in the waiting room outside of intensive care. Greg's sisters and their husbands, his brothers and wives along with Michelle's friends and our family friends and our pastor all were there. They brought us lunch to the hospital, they offered help of all kinds, they prayed with us and for us, and their presence gave us strength. We waited for Michelle to wake up and tried to reassure her that she was going to be all right. Whenever she did try to "surface" from the meds and the accident, she looked so frightened and confused, I almost preferred that she sleep. "With sleep comes healing"—we would hear that phrase many times in the coming weeks.

Doctors came and went—doctors we had never seen before—"Hello, I am the neurosurgeon that operated on your daughter;" 'Hello, I am the neurologist that will be following your daughter;" 'Hello, I am the emergency room physician that was on duty when you daughter came in." Michelle's family practice physician is also her cousin. He was at the hospital today and spent time helping us understand what had happened and what was ahead. I was glad he was there because none of the other doctors knew Michelle so how could they know how she was responding or how could they set goals for her recovery? They don't know about her hearty laugh, her sparkling eyes, her quick mind, her "mom's in charge" attitude when it involves her kids.

Greg talked about Geran needing to take Valentines to pre-school the next day and Grace needed them for Thursday so I left the hospital and picked up some Valentines, then picked up Grace at school and the other 3 at their sitter's home and we went to Michelle and Greg's home and made Valentines. Grace was old enough to help me put the kid's names on the outside of each envelope and we had them finished before Greg came to take the Grands back to the hospital to see their mom.

Greg's brothers and their families were at the hospital tonight so the Grands had friends to play with. Greg stayed at the hospital again tonight and Laura and Dirk stayed overnight with the Grands so Larry and I could get a full night's sleep. Was it only last night that we were flying home from California?

As I laid in bed trying to sleep, my mind kept returning to the hospital and all the things that we had been told today. TBI: that stands for Traumatic Brain Injury. These are 3 letters that have found a permanent location in my brain. A TBI is caused by a bump, blow or jolt to the head or a penetrating head injury that disrupts the normal function of the brain. Not all blows or jolts to the head result in a TBI. The severity of a TBI may range from mild, that is a brief change in mental status or consciousness, to severe, an extended period of unconsciousness or amnesia after the injury. The majority of TBI's that occur each year are concussions or other forms of mild TBI.[1]

Michelle is now a TBI statistic. Every year, at least 1.7 million Traumatic Brain Injuries occur either as an isolated injury or along with other injuries. TBI is a contributing factor to a third of all injury-related deaths in the United States.

Of the 1.7 million people that sustain a TBI annually, there are:

52,000 deaths

275,000 hospitalizations

1,365,000 emergency department visits [2]

My mind continued to replay the events of the last two days and I still cannot fully comprehend the magnitude of what has happened. I vow to take each day at a time and do whatever I can to help Michelle and Greg and the Grands to come through this "TBI thing" and return to their normal lives if that is possible. I talk frankly with God and ask for his help and guidance for all of us.

---

1 *2010 Nebraska Traumatic Brain Injury: Needs and Resources* Assessment Page 12 Retrieved on November 14, 2013 from www.braininjury.ne.gov/docs/10TBIassessment-ExecSum.pdf
2 *Motor Vehicle Safety* Page 1. CDC Center for Disease Control and Prevention: Retrieved on November 15, 2013 from www.cdc.gov/motorvehiclesafety

PERTINENT MEDICAL NOTES
BRYAN/LGH MEDICAL CENTER-WEST

INJURY SUMMARY:
1. Right intraventricular hemorrhage
2. Right Frontoparietal intraparenchymal hemorrhage
3. Right basal ganglia bleed
4. Recent history of seizure like events currently worked up at UNMC
5. Respiratory failure, resolved
6. Hyperglycemia

PHYSICAL THERAPY:
Treatment: Tolerated well overall. Moves left upper extremities and left lower extremities well and have normal strength. Right upper extremity is not moving much, will need to assess gait and transfers before can consider final discharge destination. Suspect possible need for rehab if has gaited or balance issues once able to be up. Will further assess strength.

SHORT TERM GOALS:
1. Patient to perform all transfers with minimal assist in 4 to 6 visits.
2. Patient to gait 420 feet X1 with minimal assist and device if needed in 4 to 6 visits.
3. Patient to go up and down steps with use of handrail and minimal to moderate assist in 6 to 8 visits.

LONG TERM GOALS:
1. Patient independent in gait and transfers by discharge from acute care.
2, Patient prepared for next level of care by discharge from acute care.

TREATMENT PLAN. See for transfers and gait twice daily

Chapter 3

Wednesday, February 13, 2008

"Mom, Check On Aidan!

MY NARRATIVE

A better morning—Michelle's breathing tube will be removed this morning and her doctors will begin to cut back on her meds so she can wake up. Greg said she had another very restless night and I offered to stay with her tonight so Greg could get some sleep. His kids also need to see him come home so their lives aren't turned upside down with both parents being out of the house. We all decided that we would get the kids back into their normal routine—Grace to first grade every day, Geran to pre-school on M-W-F mornings and all three young ones to day care on Tuesday and Thursday. Wednesday with "Grandma and Papa"--that would be Larry and me. They are used to this routine and we will try very hard to keep their lives in the same pattern.

There is no doubt they are young and do not fully understand what has happened to their mom. Grace ends up in tears every time she visits the hospital, She cries in her bed at night. Geran says he wants his dad to come home because, "I don't want him to die like mommy did." The twins continue to talk about "Mommy hit a tree," and

"Mommy can't talk." They all have lots of questions about the tubes, the neck brace, all the machines and monitors that surround Michelle's bed. They notice the patch of hair on top of her head that has been shaved. They notice that she is "sleeping." They notice that she doesn't look at them.

Aidan's broken arm has made her afraid for anyone to touch her or try to pick her up because her arm is sore whenever it is moved or bumped. Larry (Papa) is the only one she will let dress and undress her because he knows how to get her blouse off without hurting her. He also taught her to tell people, "Pick me up by my butt!" And she means it! If you start to reach for her under the arms, you get an ear full!

My friend Judy came to visit this morning. Judy is a college friend of mine. We both graduated from Nebraska Wesleyan University and were roommates in our sorority house for several years. She also lives in Lincoln so our friendship has continued for many years and it gave me such comfort and support to have her here with me during this time of crisis in our lives.

Molly, a friend of Michelle's, stopped by with her young son and we relaxed watching her toddler explore the waiting room. I should mention, Molly and Michelle also graduated from Nebraska Wesleyan University and were members of Willard Sorority as were Judy and I. Two generations together, gathered here, one to help me, and one to help Michelle but all bonded by a common college experience. Molly went in to visit Michelle and when she came out, she told me Michelle was mostly non-communicative but did smile, well, she swears Michelle almost giggled, when Molly related a funny thing that had happened, so she knew Michelle was listening and comprehending.

Our pastor arrived and asked if he could have a prayer with us and Michelle. Judy and I went in to Michelle's room and her breathing tube was gone and she looked much more comfortable. Our Pastor asked Michelle if we could pray with her and she nodded yes but did not open her eyes. When he had finished praying, Judy took Michelle's hand and said, "Michelle, this is Judy, I just came by to see you and your mom. Michelle, if there is ANYTHING we can do for you, just let me know and it will happen." Michelle opened her eyes, looked at Judy and in a very clear voice said, "Just get me out of here!" I couldn't believe it! I stayed and talked to Michelle a little more but I got no response until I said, "Michelle, I'm going to leave now and let you get some rest." She opened her eyes, looked at me and said, "Mom, check on Aidan."

Michelle had just used her "Mom's in charge" voice to say this! Sometimes when she drops off the kids to stay for a little while, she will leave instructions like, "Don't give them any treats—we are eating early tonight." Or "Change the twin's diapers, they both need dry ones." These are orders a mom gives the care givers before leaving the kids in someone else's care! And, she had just given me such a command! The astonishing thing was that Greg had decided not to tell Michelle about Aidan's broken arm, he didn't want Michelle laying there feeling guilty or worrying about Aidan. But, somewhere in her drug-induced sleep, she heard someone talk about Aidan's broken arm.

Alert to everyone reading this book—patients hear everything, even when they do not respond.

Judy stayed and helped me photograph and record the flowers Michelle had received. Since Michelle was in intensive care, the flowers were being placed on the nurse's station and soon had taken up over half of the circular counter. I knew Michelle couldn't see them so I wanted to take a picture of each arrangement so she could see them later and appreciate how many people were praying for her recovery. I also suspected that the nurses would soon ask us to begin removing the flowers since the arrangements were blocking site-lines into the Intensive Care rooms.

There were flowers from people Michelle worked with, relatives, sorority sisters, people Greg worked with, attendants in their wedding, neighbors, clients of Greg's. The nurse's station was A-Bloom! Once again the phrase, "Honey, I smell flowers" was rolling through my brain every time I entered ICC. Had it only been 48 hours ago?

Since it was Wednesday, Larry was at Greg and Michelle's house with the Grands. Larry and I have had "Grandbaby Day" each Wednesday since Grace was born. I can hardly believe there are four of them now! Starting a day at their house means getting all four up and ready so Grace can be taken to 1st grade and Geran to preschool. Back to pre-school to pick up Geran at 11:30 and back to school to pick up Grace at 3:15. This makes it hard for the twins to get a full nap in the afternoon so we are going to work on that schedule to make it easier on all of us.

Michelle became more and more awake during the day and had another round of Physical Therapy that afternoon. She is very restless and has some pain around her ankle and knee. She still has no clear idea of what happened to her. She sleeps off and on but still has trouble tracking conversations.

A high school friend stopped by over the noon hour and brought a CD of soothing sounds like the ocean waves and a mountain breeze. The nurses were able to find a CD player for us but the sound of the machines sort of overpowered the soothing ocean. I am continually amazed at how thoughtful people are and what wonderful support they have given us.

Greg went home with the Grands tonight and I stayed with Michelle at the hospital overnight. She was becoming more and more aware of her surroundings and more and more agitated about being in the hospital. The following are some of our conversations and activities during the night:

11:15 PM: Michelle removes her neck brace. Nurse came in and put it back on.

12:00 Midnight: Respiratory Therapist arrived to assist with breathing exercises. Michelle removes her neck brace.

RT: "You have to leave your brace on."

Michelle: "No--I don't"

RT: "Michelle--you have to leave your brace on."

Michelle: (Louder and more emphatically!) "No- I don't"

RT asks me to get the nurse.

Nurse: "Michelle, your doctor's orders specify that you have to wear a neck brace at all times. Do you want to be paralyzed? Do you want to be able to chase your kids and run with them? Michelle, does you neck hurt?"

Michelle: Shakes her head yes and lets them put the brace back on. She has an abrasion under her chin, probably from the air bag, so I think that is irritated when she is wearing the brace.

12:30 Michelle: "Mom, get me 2 hammers."

Mom: " I'm not exactly sure what you mean."

Michelle: "Just get me 2 hammers."

Mom: "Why do you need them?"

Michelle: "Just go tell the nurse I need 2 hammers, they'll bring them to me."

Mom: "Are you hurting?"

Michelle: "Yes."

Mom: "Is it your head?"

Michelle: "Yes."

Mom: "Is it Tylenol that you need?"

Michelle: "Yes. The nurse will bring it."

I found the nurse and delivered the message and Michelle soon got her Tylenol!

1:30 AM: Michelle removes her neck brace.

Mom: "Michelle, you need to wear this brace. Can I help you put it back on?"

Michelle: "NO!"

I go to get the nurse

Nurse: "Michelle, you have to leave this on."

Michelle: "No-I do not!"

Nurse: "Michelle, the x-rays they took of your neck are not conclusive and we don't want you to end up paralyzed. As long as you have pain, you have to wear the neck brace. Michelle, how is your neck."

Michelle: "It hurts"

Nurse: "Then you have to put on the collar."

Michelle gives in and lets the nurse put the collar back on.

2:30: Michelle takes off her neck brace and throws it to the bottom of the bed!

Mom: "Michelle, does your neck hurt?"

Michelle: "NO!!!" (She is getting smart! She has figured out that if she says it doesn't hurt, maybe she won't have to wear it.)

Mom: "Would you wear a soft one like mine." (I have a neck injury from an old pick-up accident and frequently wear a soft collar neck brace when I use the computer or when I am stitching.)

Michelle: "I don't have a soft one here."

Mom: "If I got you one, would you wear it?"

Michelle: No response.

Mom: "OK, I have to tell the nurse again that you took it off."

Nurse: "Michelle, does you neck hurt."

Michelle: "No."

Nurse: "How old are you?"

Michelle: "21" (Correct answer is 38)

Nurse: "When were you born?"

Michelle: "1969" (Correct)

Nurse: "What month is it?"

Michelle: "April." (Correct answer is February.)

Nurse: "I mean right now."

Michelle: "April."

Nurse: "Where are you?"

Michelle: "Home"

Nurse: "No, you are in the hospital. You were in a car accident. How many fingers am I holding up?"

Michelle: "5" (Correct)

Nurse: "If I were to send you a birthday card, what month should I send it?"

Michelle: Thought a long time, then: "December" (Correct answer May).

Nurse: "Do you want me to leave you alone?"

Michelle: "Yes!"

Nurse: "Does your neck still hurt."

Michelle: "NO!"

Nurse: "OK, I guess we can leave it off for now."

Michelle: Looking at me, "Why don't you put on your own neck brace now?"

3:15 AM: Michelle sits straight up and starts kicking off the covers and pulling at the cords that are coming through the opening in her robe.

Mom: "What are your doing?"

Michelle: "It's time for a shower."

Mom: "Do you feel like you need a shower?"

Michelle: "Yes, right now."

Mom: "You had one today already."

Michelle: "NO, I did not."

Mom: "They even washed your hair."

Michelle: "NO, they did not."

Mom: "Well, it is still night time. Look out the window, it is still dark. You can't take a shower in the middle of the night."

She laid back down and I straightened the sheets and she went back to sleep.

The hospital had given us a nice recliner so we could sleep by Michelle's bed. Needless to say, I got no sleep tonight! But, I certainly wasn't bored! I am fascinated by how Michelle's brain is working and how she can slip in and out of reality so quickly. It is obvious to me that her brain is trying to make connections but some of the pathways have been injured and her brain has to rebuild them.

I will find out later, that part of the healing is building new pathways! For now, I am curious about what is happening and I am taking notes because I have not been down this road before and I want to remember and understand what is happening. The term "Traumatic Brain Injury" is not part of my vocabulary and I admit, I am having trouble accepting this diagnosis.

I spend much of my evening in the recliner praying for knowledge and healing for Michelle I pray for strength for myself and my husband. I pray for Michelle's family as we all adjust our lives to help speed the healing process. *Please, God, lead us, show us how we can help the most. Lead us to those things that will help each of us cope with this sudden change in our lives.*

PERTINENT MEDICAL NOTES
BRYAN/LGH MEDICAL CENTER-WEST

OCCUPATIONAL THERAPY:

Pt upright in bed with family/friends present initially, Patient with nurse agree to shower.
Brighter affect with more facial expression.
Supine with head of bed elevated to sit edge of bed with minimal assist.
Sit to stand with minimal assist and ambulated into bathroom with minimal assist.
Still unsteady, minimal assist to shower chair.
Patient completes shower sitting on shower chair using hand held shower, questioning how she is supposed to do this, occasional cues for what to do and assist for hair and back.
Tends to drop soap with right hand.
Minimal assist to dry, minimal assist with gown.
Sit to stand with minimal assist, and minimal to stand sink side.
Oral cares--Patient initiates without putting paste on brush, cues to wipe with towel as well.
Ambulate with minimal assist back to chair, stand by assist to don socks.
Minimal assist to brush out hair with cues to avoid staples.

ASSESSMENT:

Progressing well. Rancho Level 6, still unsteady and right upper incoordination.
Agree with plan for acute rehab.

Chapter 4
Thursday, February 14, 2008
Valentine's Day

MY NARRATIVE

Today is Valentine's Day. Larry brought some Valentines the Grands had made to hang in Michelle's room. She barely looked at them. I don't think Valentine's Day even connected with her.

Thursday morning conversations:

Nurse: "Where do you live?"

Michelle: "Omaha" (Correct answer Lincoln)

Nurse: "What is your birth date?"

Michelle: "5/23" (Correct)

Nurse: "What year."

Michelle: "1969" (Correct)

Nurse: "Where are you?"

Michelle: "Midlands Hospital." (Correct answer: BryanLGH)

Nurse: "What month is it?"

Michelle: "I don't know"

Nurse: "It is February. Who it that?" (Pointing to me.)

Michelle: "That's My Mom!" (This was said with emphasis like--don't you know anything!)

After the nurse left I asked Michelle if she was hungry. She said yes, so we called for some breakfast. They brought her toast and scrambled eggs and hot tea. The toast was cut into halves and I cut it again into quarters and put a little butter on it. She picked up a piece and jammed it right into her chin.

It was very hard to watch her feel for her mouth with that piece of toast but she finally found it and put it in her mouth. I could tell she had to think about how to bite off a piece but she finally did and chewed and swallowed. This was repeated until the first quarter of toast was gone. She was worn out. I could hardly keep from picking up the toast and feeding her but something told me I had to let her do it herself so I just waited till she was ready again. By the time the toast was finished, she was bringing the piece right up to her mouth very normally and chewing was also almost normal. She sipped a little tea without spilling any and I felt like she had already conquered one challenge.

The doctors began to talk with Greg about transferring Michelle to a Rehabilitation Center. BryanLGH has its own rehab center but we live in Lincoln and it is home to one of the nationally recognized Rebab Hospitals, Madonna Rehabilitation Hospital. We asked them to check and see if Madonna had room for her. We were told they would take her on Friday as long as Michelle continued to improve.

Michelle continued to have Respiratory Therapy and Physical Therapy throughout the day and by afternoon the nurses said they were transferring her upstairs to Progressive Care. We began to separate the floral arrangements. Greg will take some home, I will take some home, some are already starting to wilt. I think to myself, "Some of us are beginning to wilt, too!"

Ah, yes, it is Valentine's day and Michelle has her best Valentine by her side, her husband Greg. They had their first date 11 years ago today! They met at a fitness gym and had visited with one another but never dated. I think the story of their first date goes something like this: Michelle had tickets to a hockey game and she asked Greg if he'd like to go! He said yes and suggested that maybe they should go to dinner first--and the rest is history!

I have noticed one interesting thing, when Greg is with her; she answers questions like her home address and the year correctly. She says their address and their phone number. When I am with her, she gives our address and our phone number and sometimes a year from when she was living with us! Maybe she gets her cues from seeing us--I don't know how she answers when none of us are here!

As I spent time by myself in the ICC waiting room, I began to gather some facts about TBI. I now know that every day in Nebraska at least one person dies from a traumatic brain injury (TBI), three people are hospitalized and over 24 people a day visit the emergency department because of TBI.

More than 300,000 people have suffered a brain injury including concussions and more than 36,527 individuals in Nebraska live with a disability caused by a traumatic brain injury.

In the last five years, there has been a steady increase in emergency department visits, hospitalizations and deaths caused by a traumatic brain injury and emergency visits for brain injury in Nebraska are higher than the national average.[3]

Why have I been to so unaware of what was happening right here in my own state? Again, I have spent my entire career in one of the medical fields and yet I don't remember seeing one diagnosis code for TBI on the many laboratory tests that have passed through my hands. I am humbled by my lack of knowledge about this "TBI thing" but I am determined to learn.

---

[3] *Nebraska Statistics: Nebraska TBI Needs and Resources Assessment Survey*: Page 1 Brain Injury Association of Nebraska retrieved on November 14, 2013.

PERTINENT MEDICAL NOTES
BRYAN/LGH MEDICAL CENTER-WEST

RADIOLOGY CONSULTATION

PATIENT NAME: S., Michelle   Date of Birth: 5/23/69   Procedure: CT head without contrast

FINDINGS: Noncontrast CT scan head is obtained and correlated with prior 2/12/08. Examination shows persisting changes in the sinuses. The posterior fossa and supratentorial space again noted to have changes of small petechial type hemorrhages in the right hemisphere primarily superiorly over the parietal distribution. Somewhat more focal hemorrhage seen posteriorly in the left hemisphere persists without change.

Impression: Stable head CT when compared to 2/12/08, 06:44 examination. Foci of hemorrhages in the right and left hemispheres seen previously persist. Gray/white matter interfaces are stable. No extraaxial processes. Intracranial pressure monitor has been removed.

Chapter 5

Friday, February 15, 2008

Watch Out For The Tricycles!

MY NARRATIVE

Michelle is moved upstairs early in the morning and she will transfer over to Madonna Rehabilitation Hospital as soon as transportation can be arranged. She and Greg took a walk this morning and her physical strength is returning. She still does not have good balance and needs a steady arm to hang onto.

Greg's sisters and their families and Melissa and I spent much of the morning at the hospital in a family waiting area near Michelle's room. She had a steady group of visitors that have not seen her before and the rest of us decided to stay out of the room and let her get a little rest before her big move!

We are all a little apprehensive about the move to Madonna but we know she needs the kind of therapy they can give her. Early diagnosis of TBI is critical for establishing rehabilitation protocols that will mean more successful recoveries. We are fortunate that Michelle's diagnosis was made at the earliest stages: the emergency medical staff that brought her in the ambulance already recognized she had a closed head injury. Many records exist of patients being released from emergency rooms because they were awake, responsive, and their physical injuries were not life-threatening. As early as 2010, The Brain Injury Association of America carried an article about research being conducted for a blood test that would provide an immediate answer as to whether the patient has sustained damage to the brain. The hope was that this blood test could also be used to diagnose concussions on the athletic fields as well as on the battlefield.[4]

Sitting here, visiting with family and friends, we realize how much Michelle has accomplished in just 5 days. Michelle was in Intensive Care Monday with a probe in her brain and by Wednesday she was taking short walks. By Thursday, she was moved from ICU to skilled care and now Friday she is transferring to Madonna. We hope and pray her progress continues at "warp-speed!"

Michelle moved to Madonna mid-afternoon and she is worn out! She is already scheduled for occupational therapy, physical therapy, and speech therapy tomorrow. We are surprised by Michelle's room, she is in the pediatric wing. That was the only room they had open. Madonna was first opened in Lincoln as a nursing home. Through the years, they have upgraded and changed till they are a fully accredited Rehabilitation Hospital.

My first thoughts when they mentioned Madonna was that I hoped there would be some people there that were Michelle's age. Well, we have little children wearing helmets driving tricycles down the corridors so I am reminded that Madonna serves all ages! Michelle will seem like the "old one" on this floor!

---

[4] Hayes, Ron PhD (Summer 2010) *"TBI in the US Military"* The Challenge: Page 5

PERTINENT MEDICAL NOTES
BRYAN/LGH MEDICAL CENTER-WEST

NURSING STAFF NOTES:

8:00 AM PT Confused regarding place and time. Inconsistent with date of accident, states accident on Valentine's Day, patient reoriented. Patient denies pain. Rt side extremities weak, Lft side strong. Pupils brisk, 3mm bilateral. Gait steady and ambulated around unit with 1 assist. Patient drowsy, follows commands. Continue to monitor and assess per plan of care.

DISCHARGE NOTES:

1. She is being dismissed to acute rehabilitation.
2. Activity is as tolerated.
   She needs to be out of bed and ambulate at least three times a day with standby assist.
3. Head of the bed 30° when in bed.
4. She is okay to shower.
5. Accu checks: will continue before meals and at bedtime. We will institute the hyperglycemia protocol.
6. Deep venous thrombosis prophylaxis including ambulating 4 X a day and sequential compression devices while in bed.
7. Fleet's or soap suds enema as needed if no bowel movement after Dulcolax.
8. She is to follow-up in the trauma outpatient clinic one week after dismissal. She is also to follow-up with neurosurgeon and neurologist per their instructions.
9. Diet as tolerated.
10. She will have physical therapy, occupational therapy, respiratory therapy evaluation upon arrival to rehabilitation. Speech will perform a cognition evaluation and treat. Continuation of her incentive spirometry every two hours while awake with nursing.
11. She is being discharged on the following medications: milk of magnesia, senna, albuterol, Pepcid, bisacodyl, sliding scale with Humalog insulin, dextrose tabs, Tylenol, and Neosporin.

Chapter 6

Saturday, February 16, 2008

"I Would Never Make a Roast!"

MY NARRATIVE

Madonna does not shut down for the weekend! Michelle was seen by a physical therapist, an occupational therapist and a speech therapist today. They are doing their initial evaluations and are surprised by some of her responses. My favorite evaluation question was from the speech therapist. Question:

"Michelle, if you were giving a dinner party for friends and you wanted to serve a roast, what time would you have to put the roast in the oven if you had a 4 pound roast and the roast baked for 15 minutes per pound and you wanted to serve the dinner at 6:00 PM. "

My smart, clever Michelle answered: "I don't really have to know that because I would never serve a roast!"

Love that girl's spunk and I'm so glad to see that it is still there!"

Physically, she is better every day. She has an "alert" monitor on her pajamas that goes off if she gets out of bed without help. She is supposed to have someone beside her at all times, especially when she goes to the bathroom. She can sit up and stand up so quickly now that it is hard to make her wait for the nurse to assist her. She does not understand why she is supposed to wait for them or even why the alarm is ringing. I am not sure she even notices the alarm at all. Greg brought the kids up today. She looks at them and smiles a little but doesn't really talk to them or even touch them. They don't interact with her very much, either, I think they feel like she's not really their "Mom!"

It suddenly occurred to me that with all that has happened to her, Michelle has not cried! Michelle is not one to cry easily, but when something is serious, the tears can flow. I know that if she realized she had totaled her car, that Aidan had broken an arm, and that she was facing some extensive therapy to return to normal, she would be crying Big Time! Her lack of tears makes me realize how much she still does not understand about the accident and how it has injured her brain and perhaps changed her life.

During the wee hours of the morning, Greg wrote "Michelle's story" on her Care Page.

Recently my wife of almost 9 years and friend of 11 years was involved in a car crash. We were leaving an appointment when she was at a stoplight behind me and her vehicle sped forward against oncoming traffic, left the road, and crashed head-on into a tree at roughly 40-50 miles an hour. The accident is being reviewed by Lincoln Police Department as to what caused the vehicle to crash. As I watched and tried to figure what was happening, I knew our lives were about to change.

We have 4 beautiful children. Gracie who is six, Geran who is four, and twin girls Aidan and Alysen who just turned three years old. The twins were in the vehicle at the time of the crash. Aidan sustained a broken left arm and bruising from the seat/lap belts. Alysen has some bruising as well but is doing great. Gracie and Geran were both at school. When I came to the vehicle and found Michelle and the twins, Michelle was breathing shortly and appeared to have been saved by the air bag. I helped Michelle clear her airway and with her breathing until help arrived. The fire and rescue team arrived and helped remove Michelle and the twins from the vehicle and we were off to Bryan Hospital-West in Lincoln, NE. Michelle sustained a severe head injury which caused bleeding and pressure to the brain tissue. A neurosurgeon drilled a small hole in Michelle's head and inserted a sensor to monitor the brain swelling. We spent the week of February 11th through the 15th praying for Michelle and she has made steady progress and is currently at Madonna Rehabilitation Hospital in Lincoln. The next steps are to help Michelle learn how to walk on her own, speak clearly, and improve her motor skills. Her memory is coming back and we are thanking God for this miracle!

About Michelle-she was born in Lincoln and graduated from East High School and Nebraska Wesleyan University. She trained at UNMC in medical technology and then got a Master's degree in Health Care Administration. In addition to managing her family, she works 3 days a week at a software development company in Lincoln, NE. The company writes software for laboratories, both data management and billing. Michelle demos their software to potential clients and assists in developing "help" screens that are associated with the programs.

We want to let CarePages.com know how glad we are to have a place like this to go to! We have been reading morning and night. Thank you.

PERTINENT MEDICAL NOTES

MADONNA REHABILITATION HOSPITAL

PHYSICAL THERAPY STAFF NOTES:

Berg Balance Test: Scale is 0-4

Sitting to Standing: 1

Standing Unsupported: 3

Sitting with Back Unsupported but Feet supported: 3

Standing to Sitting: 0

Transfers: 1

Standing Unsupported with Eyes Closed: 2

Standing Unsupported with Feet Together: 1

Reaching Forward with Outstretched Arm While Standing: 3

Pick up Object From the Floor From a Standing Position: 3

Turning to Look Behind Over Left and Right Shoulders While Standing: 2

Turn 360": 1

Place Alternate Foot on Step or Stool While Standing Unsupported: 1

Standing Unsupported One Foot in Front: 1

Standing on One Leg: 1

Total Berg Balance Score: 23 of 56

Chapter 7

Sunday, February 17, 2008

"When Hundreds are Joined in Prayer!"

MY NARRATIVE

Michelle had her best night's sleep last night. She only woke up once from a tickle in her throat that left her coughing. Laura, her sister, stayed with her last night. Since it is Sunday, Laura (a pastor) had a little Sunday service just for the two of them--a hymn and a prayer! Michelle took a shower and washed her hair and even put on some makeup herself.

Larry and I went to 8:00 AM church today. Our church has a tradition that a lay person gives the prayer after the offering is taken. It was my Sunday to give the prayer and I felt it was important for me to do that. God had already answered many prayers for us this week and I needed to thank him in person, in our church. The following is my prayer:

> *Our Father God, We bring our gifts today in gratitude for the love you shower upon us each and every day. This week we have been humbled once again by the power of prayer that you have shown us. We have seen first hand the healing of both body and spirit and we have witnessed the strength that comes from You when hundreds join together in prayer. We ask for special blessings on our church family this week and we ask that you use our gifts to continue to spread your word throughout our community, our nation, and our world. Guide and direct and make us grateful in all things. In Jesus name we pray. Amen*

Well, I can't say I made it through the prayer very easily, I finished with a shaky voice and a few tears! After church was over, many people in church came to ask about Michelle and find out how she was doing and ask how they could help. Of course many were already praying for Michelle and her family. One person told me she was the mom of one of Michelle's high school classmates and that she had called him the day after the accident. He lives on the east coast and she wanted him to know what happened to Michelle. He told her that one of their classmates had e-mailed him after the accident and they already had a prayer chain started with all of the classmates that lived on the east coast. Somehow I knew that "hundreds were joined together in prayer" but it was wonderful to have that confirmed!

By afternoon, Michelle's blood pressure was very low and they had to take her down for her therapies in a wheel chair. We will talk to her doctor about her meds tomorrow. I think she is taking too much of something! In speech therapy they worked on recalling. She would have to read a paragraph, then they would ask her questions about what she read. They also reviewed with her what she had done in the other therapies today. They did some eye tests and discovered that her eyes hurt when she looks up. Her peripheral vision on the left side is not as good as the right. She was able to give her kids names and their ages and the correct address of her home. The sessions wear her out and she takes nice naps in between them.

After one trip to the bathroom, she came out and said, "Let's just eat lunch here and then go home." Boy! Don't I wish that were possible!

In Physical Therapy they had the following conversation:

Therapist: "Where do you live?"

Michelle: "Lincoln"

Therapist: "Where?"

Michelle: "Near here."

Therapist: "What street?"

Michelle: "Sycamore"

Therapist to Mom: "Is that right?"

Mom: "It was right for most of her life but now it's Burr Oaks Road."

Michelle: "Oh yes, that's right. It's way south of here!"

During the night she woke and said; "I want to trend way." I finally figured out she wanted to turn over.

Once in the evening she got up and went into the bathroom and stood by the sink. I asked her what she was doing and she said: "I am heating my pizza."

Brain injury is unpredictable in its consequences. Brain injury affects who we are, the way we think, act, and feel. It can change everything about us in a matter of seconds. There are **Cognitive Consequences, Physical consequences** and **Emotional Consequences.**

Cognitive Consequences can include:

- Short term memory loss, long term memory loss
- Slowed ability to process information
- Trouble concentrating or paying attention for periods of time
- Difficulty keeping up with a conversation, other communication difficulties such as word finding problems
- Spatial disorientation (balance)
- Organizational problems and impaired judgment
- Unable to do more than one thing at a time
- A lack of initiating activities, or once started, difficulty in completing tasks without reminders

Michelle is having most of these difficulties at this time. The doctors have told us that she suffered multiple hemorrhages in her brain and also has some frontal lobe damage from the brain hitting the inside of the skull when her car hit the tree.

Physical Consequences Can Include:

- Seizures of all types
- Muscle spasticity
- Double vision or low vision, even blindness
- Loss of smell or taste
- Speech impairments such as slow or slurred speech
- Headaches or migraines
- Fatigue, increased need for sleep
- Balance problems

Michelle experienced the last 4 of these consequences but not the first 4.

Emotional Consequences:

    Increased anxiety

    Depression and mood swings

    Impulsive behavior

    More easily agitated

    Egocentric behaviors; difficulty seeing how behaviors affect others [5]

Michelle experienced all of these consequences.

The doctors and nurses and rehabilitation staff assure us that all the consequences will improve and slowly disappear as Michelle's brain heals and their therapies assist her in recovering. I understand more and more that this "TBI thing" does not have a quick cure and we must be patient and we must help Michelle be patient.

PERTINENT MEDICAL NOTES
MADONNA REHABILITATION HOSPITAL

NURSING STAFF NOTE:

15:15 PM Assumed care. Patient alert, forgetful, perseverates on feeling hot/cold intermittently. Fan, covers, on/off, Room door open/closed. Vital signs and physical data collected and were normal. Burr hole in top of head is dry, approximated with staples, no redness or edema. Noted abrasions/scabbed areas under chin, right ankle, left knee. No complaints of pain earlier this shift. Transfers with one assist gait is unsteady. Continent of urine. Patient husband here and other visitors throughout shift. Out to dining area for supper, feeds self.

---

[5] 'Living with Brain Injury: The Consequences of Brain Injury." Page 2 Brain Injury Association of Nebraska. Retrieved on November 14, 2013 at www.biane.org/what/

Chapter 8

Monday, February 18, 2008

A Bedside Manicure and Pedicure

MY NARRATIVE

Has it really been a week since the accident? In some ways it seems like it has only been a few days, other times it seems like weeks since we flew to California. Larry and Greg went with Michelle to therapies today. Since Larry is a physical therapist, he was anxious to see how she was doing during her therapy sessions. In speech therapy they worked on math/time concepts and again Michelle had to read a paragraph and the therapist asked her questions about what she had read. They are testing her recall. In Physical Therapy, they worked on standing, balance and walking in the halls. A psychologist visited with her today and quizzed her again about time and place, family, memory, and math problems. These all work together to challenge the brain to rebuild itself into the fully functioning organ that it had been.

Occupational therapy had her walk down to a full kitchen designed for rehab patients. She was supposed to make muffins and Larry and Greg were both freaked out by her reaction to the kitchen. I will go into detail about that in tomorrow's OT session.

In the afternoon PT session, she again walked to and from the gym and while there practiced going up and down steps and rode the stationary bike for 10 minutes. In speech therapy, there was more logic and deductive reasoning puzzles this afternoon. The occupational therapist again evaluated her vision and recommended that she go to the Vision Clinic and be tested by an eye doctor that specializes in traumatic brain injuries and how they affect the eyes.

It is not uncommon for patients that suffer TBI to have vision problems, in fact most literature says 20-40 percent of people with TBI experience related vision disorders. According to Dr. Gregory Goodrich, Program Coordinator for the Optometric Research Fellowship Program at the VA hospital in Palo Alto, CA, the two most common kinds of visual problems are Visual Acuity Loss and Visual Field Loss. Visual Acuity Loss is caused from damage to the eye itself and Visual Field Loss is caused by damage to the nerve fibers that carry visual signals from the eyes to the brain. A full visual examination should be done on any TBI patient suffering any type of eye pain for visual impairment. [6]

I am relieved that they can follow up with the eye pain Michelle describes whenever she rolls her eyes upward. There is an eye clinic right here in Madonna and they will be able to test her sight this week.

Michelle was exhausted by mid afternoon. While she was sleeping, one of the neurologist's on staff at Madonna came to check on her. I asked him about the meds and told him I thought she was on too much of something for her height and weight. He agreed and decided to stop all meds that she came with from the hospital so they could get a good evaluation of how many of her symptoms--especially the low blood pressure--was from meds and how many were from the accident. He also wants a second EEG to see if activity in the frontal lobe indicates susceptibility to seizures. She will have this Wednesday morning.

The highlight of the day was when my nephew's wife, Linda and their daughter, Dana, came to Madonna and gave Michelle a manicure and pedicure! She slept off and on but I could tell it really relaxed her to have her hands and feet massaged and she was especially happy to have her toenails polished since she spends most of her time barefooted.

---

[6] McDonough, Victoria Tilney, BrainLine February 2010 : *"Vision Issues After Brain Injury: BrainLine talks with Dr. Gregory Goodrich.* Retrieved on March 28, 2010 from www.brainline.org/content/2010/02/vision-issues-after-brain-injury-brainline-talks-with-Dr-Gregory-Goodrich

It is important to bring some things from home that reminds your patient of their "other" life. We brought Michelle a picture of the Grands together. She always knew their names and ages whenever the nurses or therapists asked her about the picture. We brought some of her soft pajamas and sweat shirts and other comfy clothes that she liked to hang out in. We wanted her to have some things that were not "hospital" related to keep reminding her of the life she was struggling to recapture.

PERTINENT MEDICAL NOTES
MADONNA REHABILITATION HOSPITAL

PHYSICIANS PROGRESS NOTES:

ASSESSMENT AND PLAN:

1. A 38 year old female with history of mild traumatic brain injury. I discussed further with the patient's family today. Apparently she has had multiple syncopal episodes over the last six years. She has had extensive workup including continuous EEG monitoring and has not been found to have any seizure activity. In view of the fact that she is having issues with hypotension, nausea, excessive sleepiness, and difficulty tolerating therapies, will discontinue Dilantin at this time.

2. Will simplify other medication regimens and as blood sugars have been normal, will discontinue sliding scale insulin and Accu checks and will also discontinue Dulcolax.

Chapter 9

Tuesday, February 19, 2008

Let's Make Cookies

MY NARRATIVE

I stayed with Michelle Monday night and plan to be with her Tuesday during her therapies. She had a pretty good night but twice got up and was in the bathroom before I could wake up enough to stop her or have her wait for the nurse. They staff did always get there in time to help her back to bed but she really moves fast once she decides to get up!

Greg came in early this morning and had questions for Michelle.

Greg: "Do we do online banking?"

Michelle: "Yes."

Greg: "How do I get online, do I need a password?"

Michelle: "Yes, it is my social security number."

Greg: "What is that?"

At this point Michelle repeated her Social Security number to him 2 or 3 times while he tried to enter it in his new Blackberry so he would have it with him when he got home. They went through the same thing with the password. She had to repeat it to him several times till he got it typed in correctly. She knew the correct answers immediately and could explain the steps he needed to do to pay bills online. I thought this was a good sign and a great way to start the day!

Michelle had speech therapy and completed a check book register. She does not have any trouble with math or numbers. She also located items in the local paper and the therapist made a note that she needed to work on attending to details.

Physical therapy included walking back and forth to the gym. While at the gym, she worked on establishing baseline exercises and cardiovascular work. She rode the stationery bike pretty well and also worked on climbing steps.

Our last therapy stop in the morning was to the kitchen at Madonna with a goal of making cookies. The therapist asked her if she had made cookies before and she nodded yes. Actually, making cookies with my girls is something we had done all the time they were growing up. I prided myself in never buying cookies. If we had cookies, they were always homemade.

The therapist handed her a "mix" for cookies and told her to read it and get the things she needed. She only needed an egg and water so the therapist helped her find the egg and the measuring cup. There was already a mixing bowl and mixing spoon on the counter for her to use. The therapist told her to go ahead and make the dough.

Michelle picked up the package of cookie dough mix and used her fingers across the top of the mix as though her fingers were a scissors. She then turned the mix upside down over the bowl and tapped it a few times as though she was making sure all the mix had fallen out of the bag. Next, she picked up the egg and gently touched it to the side of the bowl and then made a motion with the egg as though she was opening the egg and dropping the yolk and white onto the mix. She set the egg back very gently on the counter. She next pretended to pick up the measuring cup and walked over to the sink, made a motion of turning on the water and continued the motion of holding the non-existent measuring cup under the dry water faucet! She checked the level of the non-existent water and then walked over and made the motion of dumping the water into the bowl.

Last, she picked up the mixing spoon and begin to stir the "nothingness" in the bowl. The therapist asked her what she was doing. Michelle answered, "Mixing up the cookie dough." The therapist picked up the bowl and turned it over and banged it on the counter and said, "Nope, Michelle, there is nothing in here!"

Michelle looked bewildered and frightened. I DID NOT CRY! My heart still skips a beat when I talk about this. This child of mine had made cookies by my side all of her life. She had only done online banking for a few years. Yet, she remembered how to tell her husband the way to get online but she didn't even realize she wasn't making cookies. They had told us she would have short term memory problems but making cookies was definitely in her long term memory. I was shocked at what I had just witnessed.

The trauma of that therapy session was not yet over. Under the therapist's guidance, she finally got the egg and the water in the dough and mixed it up. She did remember how to make the cookies, dropping each piece of dough onto the cookie sheet and making nice straight rows. (Yes, momma always taught her girls to make nice straight rows so the cookies had room to raise!) The trauma came when the oven timer rang and she opened the oven door and reached in to get the cookies without grabbing a hot pad!!! The therapist was right there and grabbed her hand, but if she hadn't, Michelle would have reached in and picked up the hot cookie sheet. I DID NOT CRY!!! Michelle was not going to see me cry today! I saved that for the drive home.

I now know there is a term for the phenomena that I refer to as "phantom actions." Michelle believes she is doing something but she is only going through the motions, not actually performing the task. It is called Agnosia and it means "lack of awareness" or "the loss of ability to comprehend the meaning of objects." Her brain is going through the motions but she is totally unaware that she is not actually doing them. Once again I have been caught completely off guard and witnessed something I did not expect. I still have so much to learn about this "TBI thing"... the 3 little letters that I have so much trouble saying!

Michelle had speech and physical therapy again in the afternoon. It was a long day for both of us. Greg took Aidan to the doctor again today. The doctor said Aidan will know when it is time to take off the sling and whenever she is ready to take it off, she can. He wants to check it again in a month but says it is healing perfectly.

Michelle's babysitter and I decided one of our gifts to Michelle was to have the twin's potty trained by the time Michelle came home from Madonna. Michelle had been going to train them when they turned 3 but had not yet started. I figured they were old enough to learn quickly so I bought some thick training panties and put them on! We only had a few accidents! We had many trips to the potty because one or the other would think they had to go and then only a few tinkles! But, her babysitter helped immensely and we were soon ready to switch to regular panties. This weekend I will take them to the shopping center and let them pick out whichever "big girl panties" they want.

Today's therapies have been very reflective of the type of care a TBI patient should be receiving: 2 physical therapy treatments per day, 2 occupational therapy treatments per day, 2 speech therapy treatments per day, care team composite plan and goals for discharge. Even though the therapists mentioned frequently that Michelle was tired or fatigued, the treatments continued. It's very important in a brain injury that retraining the brain begins as quickly as possible and is as intense as possible to stimulate the brain to heal itself.

If you are helping select a rehabilitation center, appropriate questions for you to ask would be:

How many therapy treatments will be given each day?
How many different types of therapy will be given each day?
What's the estimated length of time for each therapy that is given?
Is neuropsychology part of the treatment plan?
How often are team meetings planned to keep the family informed of progress?

There is much more information about selecting a Rehabilitation Center in the Appendix of this book.

PERTINENT MEDICAL NOTES
MADONNA REHABILITATION HOSPITAL

CARE PLAN TEAM COMPOSITE:

PLAN DISCHARGE GOAL/DATE:

> This patient was admitted to Madonna Rehabilitation Hospital Acute Rehab unit on 2/15/08. Patient was a transfer from BryanLGHWest. Patient was in a motor vehicle accident on February 11, 2008. She suffered a complicated mild traumatic brain injury from this accident and now has been transferred to an Acute Rehab level of care. The team has estimated she will need an approximate two week length of stay making her approximate discharge date March 1, 2008.

GOALS:
> 1. Patient will complete self-care's independently with adaptive equipment as needed.
> 2. Patient will complete slight homemaking, activities independently.
> 3. Patient will require standby assist with childcare activities for one hour.
> 4. Patient will demonstrate increased muscle strength by 10 pounds for independence with meal prep.
> 5. Patient will perform bed mobility independently.
> 6. Patient will perform functional transfers independently.
> 7. Patient will be able to ambulate greater than 1000 feet without adaptive device independently.
> 8. Patient will have increased BERG space balance score of greater than 45 out of 56. 9. Patient will be able to ascend/descend a flight of stairs with a handrail independently.
> 10. Patient will demonstrate characteristics of a Rancho Los Amigos level VIII.

Chapter 10

Wednesday, February 20, 2008

A 3:00 A.M. Wake-up Call

MY NARRATIVE

    This day started off with a wake up call at 3:00 am to get Michelle ready for the EEG she had scheduled at Bryan Hospital. They had her shower and wash her hair to stay awake. I was staying with her so I had to help keep her awake. They said they needed her to be sleep-deprived for the EEG as it would be more accurate. Greg picked her up at 7:45. The temperature was 2 degrees with a wind chill of 15-20 below. When they got to the hospital the tech said, "Oh, she didn't need to be sleep-deprived for this!!!! The EEG took most of the morning but Greg rewarded her with a hot chai tea on the way back to Madonna! That perked her up and raised her spirits!

    I did not go with her to all her therapies today. I visited with her neurologist and asked if we needed to keep staying overnight with her at the hospital. He said no, her room is right by the nurse's station and they can see in her room at all times. The bed Greg or I have to sleep on is one that pulls out of an upholstered chair. We both have trouble even sleeping at all so I think we are going to try to let her be on her own at night.

Once she returned from her EEG, the therapies began again. In Occupational Therapy they worked on making grocery lists and visually locating the things on her list. Physical Therapy noted that she was very tired so they worked on visual trials. They noted she had visual perceptual/spatial difficulties and they are glad she is scheduled for the vision clinic tomorrow. Speech therapy went well with Michelle completing logic/deductive/reasoning puzzles. Therapist noted, "You did pretty well!" She also listened to articles and answered comprehension questions. She was too tired to read the articles so the therapist read them and she was still able to answer the questions. This is good!

About eleven o'clock at night, Greg called us and asked if we could go back to Madonna. Michelle kept getting up out of bed and trying to leave the wing of the rehab center and they had to get a net cage and put it on her bed to keep her in. We agree with Greg that this is probably going to freak her out so we headed over to Madonna. We found Michelle sleeping peacefully--actually better than most other nights. We stayed with her an hour and finally left. We decided maybe this was giving her some security or boundaries that made her feel secure. Boy, were we wrong about that, but **we** slept well that night!

PERTINENT MEDICAL NOTES
MADONNA REHABILITATION HOSPITAL

RESTRAINT FLOW RECORD:
Patient irritable, continually trying to get out of bed without using call light. Confused, thinks husband is outside her window. Net bed applied at 21:15. Family notified

PHYSICIANS ORDERS: RESTRAINT ORDER SET
21:00 PM: Reason for Restraint: Patient exhibits the following:
1. Impaired decision-making and is unable to understand the benefits, risks, and alternatives for medical treatments being conducted and requires restrictive intervention.
2. Patient has decreased level of consciousness or altered mental status, and is unable to remember and follow instructions, shows a vague awareness of self and body.
3. Patient demonstrates generalized or shallow agitation for aggression, sudden impulsive behaviors, impaired memory or ability to follow directions, or wondering secondary to brain injury, and requires restrictive intervention to prevent injury to self and others.

TYPE OF RESTRAINT: NETBED
Purpose of Restraint:
1. Minimize risk of falling due to unsafe ambulation (i.e., poor balance, weakness)
2. Minimize risk of falling out of bed.

Chapter 11
Thursday, February 21, 2008
Grace's Lunch Money Windfall

MY NARRATIVE

Thursday was a good day. Michelle worked with OT on sequencing home management tasks, visual perception to locate items and dynamic balance. In PT, she used the NU step for 17 minutes and walked the hallways during breaks. OT worked again with her on visual scanning at Dynavision, on divided attention tasks, and practiced accessing a community bathroom, toileting, and hand washing. Afternoon PT noted she was sleeping very soundly and they had trouble waking her up but they did go back to the gym where she used the NU Step for 10 minutes and worked on side to side balance. In Speech Therapy, they reviewed her memory book and talked about solutions to various situational problems.

Michelle keeps asking to go home (or demanding!) and so I met with her Rehab team to find out what needed to be accomplished before she goes home.

Occupational Therapy says she has to be able to do independent self care, light housekeeping, improved muscle strength, and she has to be able to read 15 pages without her vision becoming blurred. They also have to observe her for 1 hour with her children.

Physical Therapy says she has to be independent in all her movements. She has to be able to move from bed to chair, she has to be ambulatory 1000 feet, her balance test has to be at least of score of 56 (right now hers is 45) and she has to be able to go up and down steps while holding onto 1 handrail.

Speech Therapy says she has to score a Rancho VIII before she goes home, right now she is a Rancho VI-VII. They are estimating 2-3 weeks with either some outpatient therapy or home health following dismissal. The hospital also wants to put me in touch with Brain Trauma Injury support groups. I am not ready yet!

In the afternoon, Michelle had her appointment with the eye doctor at the vision clinic within Madonna. Her appointment was for 3:00 but she insisted on going down at 2:45. I was reluctant because she is so impatient but I had to follow her once she set out on her own. She kept walking up to the door and opening it even though they told her we would need to wait outside the door until 3:00. She did this at least 3 times. I tried sitting on chairs outside the room but she would just "bound" out the them and head for the door, grabbing it before I could grab her.

I finally suggested that we wait just outside the door so we could go in as soon as it opened. We stood there about 5 minutes and she looked at me with this "lost little girl" look. I said, "Michelle, are you tired?" She shook her head yes. I said, "Just lean here on my shoulder for a little while and then they will open the door." She reached for me and laid her head on my shoulder and we stood and I held her close until the door opened. It felt so good to me-my first hug since the accident. This is my baby and she is hurting, she is lost and scared, and I pray she is getting comfort from my arms around her, holding her securely. *Dear Lord, I first need to thank you for all the healing that has already occurred. But, you can see how frightened she is. Let my strength flow into her, let her feel my love and support. Help her know that she is getting better.* I knew she was frightened standing there, not understanding what she should do. She does not understand the concept of waiting! *Lord, will you just let this door open!* The door opened and her eye exam began. *Thanks!*

Michelle had no trouble reading any of the eye charts. Her eyes just hurt when she looks up. The doctor thought that if the therapists could do some more exercises with eye therapy, her pain would be gone soon. She did not believe Michelle had any lasting eye damage from the accident. We needed some good news like this!

Greg asked me to visit with her employer and find out if the company had disability insurance and family medical leave. He is already overwhelmed with hospital bills and car insurance and 4 kids so I was glad to help and I called her company.

I was able to make an appointment with the Human Resources department where Michelle works. One of the owners of the company joined us in the meeting. The company does have disability insurance that kicks in after 6 months. The owner told me to assure Michelle that they will continue her salary until the disability insurance kicks in. We are all hoping she will be back at work long before then but I was so pleased and surprised to hear them say they would continue her salary until she returned to work. I believe it was a very generous offer and I wonder how many other companies would do that. They also assured me that Michelle would always have a position in their company. She was hired in the early years of their company's development and they said we could assure her that her job was secure.

As I was leaving the meeting, Michelle's boss called me aside and told me she was following up on all of Michelle's e-mails. She told me that an e-mail had come from the school saying Grace's lunch account was out of money and additional funds should be added to the account. She told me she had driven over to the school and added $20.00 to the account. She didn't want to bother Greg or any of us with such a "small" thing, so she just took care of it. I offered to reimburse her but she was actually insulted and said, "No, that was just a small thing I could do to help. I was glad I could do something to help you out."

When I told Greg, he told me there had been a message on their answering machine at home regarding Grace's school lunch money account so he had run over the next day and added $20.00 to the account.

I related this story to my oldest daughter, Laura, and she told me when she had gone to school the first day to pick up Grace, she had gone to the office and introduced herself and told them about Michelle's accident and they mentioned Grace's lunch money account so Laura gave them $20.00. She didn't mention it to Greg or to us because, again, she didn't want to bother the family with such trivia and she was glad she could do something to help!

Grace's lunch money account was sufficient to the end of the school year! I was reminded again how generous people are and how much they are willing to do to help.

Greg brought the kids over to Madonna tonight and brought supper with him. We all ate at a big table outside her room. Michelle looks at the kids and smiles at them but doesn't really talk to them and when she is done eating, she goes back to her room and crawls in bed. They seem to accept that she is not going to talk to them and they found books for Larry and I to read to them while Greg visited with Michelle. I was worried about the kid's reaction to Michelle's net bed but their Dad is so smart--he told them mommy had a "bouncy pit" bed. They thought it was pretty cool but the little ones wondered why they couldn't bounce in it! Grace and Geran know something is wrong with their mom, so they keep their distance.

Michelle's reaction to the kids has been a surprise to me. She talks about being anxious to see them, but when they are here, she hardly pays any attention to them. There are no hugs, no questions about their day, no interest in staying with them and or watching them, That is definitely not the norm for Michelle. I am wondering if her brain is so focused on healing itself internally, that everything else is pushed to a "later" category.

Life changes for everyone after a TBI. For all persons suffering a TBI and for all of their families, there are stages of recovery. I attended the 7th Annual Brain Injury Conference in Nebraska in 2013. One of the speakers talked about the changes that occur in families when there is a TBI injury. The speaker defined these changes as Adjustment, Coping and Acceptance. Since each brain injury is different, each recovery period is different. Research has shown that there are some Key Factors which impact each step of the recovery. These factors are:

Pre-injury lifestyle of the family

Locations of the injury or injuries in the brain

Pre-injury lifestyle of the patient.

Stages of Recovery for the Family

Stage 1: 1-3 months: Shock of injury, Hopes for Full Recovery, Denial of Severity

Stage 2: 3-18 months: Recognition of Severity, Helplessness, Frustration

Stage 3: 6-24 months: Possible annoyance with survivor,
    Family expects full independence,
    Starts to recognize the reality of improvement,
    Starts seeking information about TBI

Stage 4: 10-24 months: Reality sets in, Family exhausted,
    Redirection of time with loved ones.
    Bereavement-like emotions may occur.

Stage 5: 12-24 months: Profound sadness, Family begins to grieve again,
    Mourns loss of personality

Stage 6: 2-3 years: Greater understanding, Understanding person may never be the same,
    Begin to accept, Begins to address needs of entire family.

Stages of Recovery for the Patient

Since each brain injury is unique, no length-of-time estimates are given for the stages of recovery.

Stage 1: Denial that recovery won't occur, Denial of past and current limitation, Avoidance of referral to rehabilitation,

Stage 2: Grieving over personal losses, Helplessness, Sadness, Sorrow, Anger.

Stage 3: Depression, Limited control over life, Loneliness, Anger

Stage 4: Guilt, Accident their fault, Believes families now blames the patient.

Stage 5: Coping Skills begin to emerge, Displacement, Regression, Intellectualization

Stage 6: Acceptance. Gains new perspective on living, Makes mental decisions to live with reality, Renegotiates with old relationships, Redefines self. [7]

Michelle is definitely in denial at this stage of her recovery. She does not talk about her therapies or rehabilitation. She talks endlessly about going home and doesn't recognize her impairments at this time. She is getting physically stronger and her brain is definitely beginning to plot and plan how she can get home and return to her normal life. Of course, she thinks she is ready right now.

PERTINENT MEDICAL NOTES
MADONNA REHABILITATION HOSPITAL

PHYSICIAN PROGRESS NOTES:

ASSESSMENT AND PLAN:
1. Traumatic brain injury. Continue physical therapy and occupational therapy for mobility and self-care and speech therapy and neuropsychology for cognitive and behavioral issues.
2. Patient is demonstrating some increasing impulsivity particularly in the evenings and last night I was contacted by nursing about 6 PM. We did proceed with the Net bed and I do suspect this is mainly because arousal has improved off the Dilantin.
3. Awaiting results of EEG done on Tuesday.
4. Check labs tomorrow including CBC and comprehensive metabolic panel.
5. Will ask neuropsychology to provide counseling and support for patient's husband who is having difficulty adjusting to the situation.

---

[7] Gurreridge, Debroah, MS, CBIS, Kansas City, MO. April 4, 2013. *"Different Faces of Brain Injury: Adjustment, Coping and Accepting."* 7th Annual Nebraska Brain Injury Conference. Kearney Nebraska Convention Center, Kearney, NE April 4 & 5, 2013, Lecture

Chapter 12
Friday, February 22, 2008
"Let's Go, Mom!"

MY NARRATIVE

Today was another moving day for Michelle. Madonna moved her to a different room on this floor because it has a door that will keep her from wandering through the halls. She has an ankle bracelet and whenever she opens the door that would give her access to the hallway, an alarm rings.

She did all of her therapies today. Physical Therapy: NU-Step Bike, standing balance and coordination tests. Speech Therapy: time concept story problems, making inferences from information read, worked on problem solving and determining cause/effect, multistep time problems. Occupational Therapy: worked on activities of daily living.

I came to see her in the afternoon. She was sitting on her bed with the cage unzipped and she looked me very clearly in the eye with a sweet little smile on her face, and said, "Let's go, Mom!" I said: "OK, where do you want to go." She said: "Let's walk." She jumped off the bed and looked physically very strong and we walked out of the room and she immediately turned right and went straight to a door that was an emergency exit. She started to push the panic bar that you would open in case of fire, I told her we couldn't go down those steps. She said, "Yes, we're going out to the car and you are taking me home." I told her I couldn't do that, she wasn't ready yet.

We turned around and went through the ward door. I pushed the alarm button and we went through and walked down the hallway and she turned immediately toward another emergency exit and we had the same conversation. I had a hard time keeping her walking without heading for a door. When we came back, the nurse asked me if I felt she was an escape risk. I said, "Yes, for sure, you have to keep an eye on her because the temperature is below O outside and she doesn't know enough to even put a coat on. Don't trust her walking the halls by herself, for a minute." It was hard for me to say that about Michelle but she was very determined and was getting physically stronger every day and her actions with me today showed me that she would bolt if she got the chance.

One of the psychologists came to get her late in the afternoon and took her down to her office to do an evaluation. About 20 minutes later, Michelle came back into the room. The psychologist soon followed and explained that Michelle wouldn't finish the test. I asked her why not.

Michelle: "Mom, the questions are stupid, anyone could do them, it is a waste of my time."

Psychologist: "Michelle, we need a baseline, we need to see where you are now so when we test you again we can see what progress you have made."

Michelle: "But the questions are so easy and so stupid, I don't know how you can figure out anything from them. Anyone could answer them."

Mom: "Michelle, they give this test to everybody. It helps them evaluate how long people need to be in therapy and what kind of therapies they may need. Since it is so easy for you, you would be helping them set up a baseline for others."

Michelle: "I'm tired and I just don't want to be there another 40 minutes."

Mom: "How about if I go with you and when you get tired, we'll just come back."

Michelle: "OK, but I'll probably want to come right back."

Mom: "I just hope you can try to finish it so they can use it to help other people,"

We went back to the psychologist's office and she finished the test. The psychologist fussed that it was really supposed to be done all at one time and since there was a break during the test, it might not be valid! Well, at least she finished it and hopefully it will produce some meaningful information.

PERTINENT MEDICAL NOTES
MADONNA REHABILITATION HOSPITAL

NEUROPSYCHOLOGICAL SCREENING REPORT

NAME: S., Michelle   AGE: 38 years   EDUCATION: 15 years;   DOMINANCE: right

IMPRESSION:

At this time, Michelle's neuropsychological testing results reveal significant impairment across all areas that were assessed. Given her premorbid status, as a successful professional, these testing results suggest severe difficulty, likely a result of her recent brain injury. Taking into consideration her decreased motivation and cooperation throughout the task, Michelle still exhibits neuropsychological deficits based on clinical observations throughout her inpatient hospital stay. Although these scores are probably not an accurate representation of her current status, they do reflect some areas of impairment that are of concern. In particular, given Michelle severe attention and concentration and visuospatial skills, she should not be left at home alone without 24 hour supervision. She should not resume driving or return to work until physician has instructed her to do so.

Chapter 13

Saturday, February 23, 2008

"Alice . . . Betty . . . Carol"

MY NARRATIVE

Saturday was a quiet day. Michelle is on a new prescription anti-seizure med for her injuries to the frontal lobe of the brain. They have finally diagnosed her as having a "moderate" brain trauma. The medication makes her really tired and out of touch. The doctors will review the dosage again and see if they can lower it or find another one so she is more alert.

She had lots of company today and Larry took her on several long walks. Greg's sister went along to shut off alarms as they wandered in and out of the long corridors at this rehabilitation hospital. She took a couple of good naps and told me to go get her some new clothes because all her old ones were just hanging on her. She has lost 25 pounds since the accident and she looks like a teenager again.

She just had shortened therapies today. She is becoming more uncooperative and talks endlessly about going home. The therapists are very good at distracting her and changing therapy a little to adapt to her mood changes. In late afternoon, the speech therapist came to see her. Michelle had been sleeping very well and just couldn't wake up and couldn't stay awake to read so the therapist told her to use the alphabet and give a girls name in alphabetical order for each letter of the alphabet. Michelle didn't open her eyes or respond so the therapist asked her again. My daughter Melissa and her husband were with me and we looked at each other and I think we were all ready to tell the therapist to leave and come back later when all of a sudden we heard, "Alice.... Betty....Carol.... Diana....Evelyn....Faith...slowly, softly, on and on to the Z's. She just couldn't think of a Z name and finally said "Zeus!" Melissa and I cheered and I told the therapist to be sure to mark that off her check list as "completed!"

Michelle still has not cried! All the rest of us have cried, but not Michelle. I know she does not realize the scope of what has happened to her. I know she would cry about Aidan's broken arm, her own totaled car. I know once she can comprehend what has happened, she will cry. That will be the sign that her "accident brain" is reconnecting to her "real brain."

This evening, Melissa and Jason had a little get-together with friends at their town house. We brought the "Grands" over while Greg stayed at the hospital with Michelle. Melissa and Jason have a dining room table that is tall with tall chairs to go with it. Of course, the "Grands" all wanted to sit on the BIG chairs but getting up and down off them was not easy for the 3-year olds, Aidan and Alysen. About the third time Aidan told Papa she wanted to get down, Larry was too slow for her so she took off her sling and threw it on the ground and proceeded to get down by herself. She announced, "See, I don't need this anymore." It had only been 12 days since the accident and we thought maybe she was pushing it a little but Larry sat down with her and showed her some exercises that would help make her arm strong again. She could do them all without pain so the days of "Pick me up by my Butt!" are over!

PERTINENT MEDICAL NOTES
MADONNA REHABILITATION HOSPITAL

SPEECH THERAPY STAFF NOTE

> 3:00 PM Patient was seen at bedside with family members present. Therapies focused on reading and recall at paragraph level, attention. Patient's mother reported that patient had started a new medication and has been sleeping most of the day. Patient awakened for therapies and remained drowsy throughout session. Read moderate-length articles on familiar topics and answered content questions 80%. Patient efficiently located answers in text for items missed. Long passages with less familiar content needed moderate to maximum cues. Attention maintained throughout alphabet when patient efficiently gave names for every letter in order.

Chapter 14

Sunday, February 24, 2008

More "Phantom" Actions

MY NARRATIVE

Greg and I took the kids to church today and then went to Madonna to see Michelle. When we got there, we found Michelle in the lobby with Larry and visitors--mostly Greg's family. Michelle visited with them for maybe 5 minutes, answered a couple of questions, then just got up and walked back to her room and crawled in bed. She never said a word, just got up and left.

The family had gathered in a lounging area on the first floor and Michelle had to use the elevator or climb the stairs to find her way back to the room by herself. She did this with no trouble but it bothers me that she appears to have no interest in visitors or visiting!

After a nice nap, she got up and found Greg and the kids for a little while, then the same thing, got up and went to the room and crawled in bed. She didn't sleep, just laid there and looked at the wall. I can tell her mind is working--or she is trying very hard to figure out how she got here, why she's here, and what her future is holding. I think that is all she's able to focus on at this time. She wants so badly to understand what is happening.

Everyone was gone and it was time for supper. Michelle was still dozing on and off and since she had slept a good part of the day, I suggested she get up and sit in her chair and wait for her food to be brought to her room. They usually serve about 5:30 and it was 5:15 so I thought food would be there soon. At 5:45 the food had still not been delivered and I looked over at her and she was doing her little "phantom eating thing" using her finger like a spoon and picking up food off an imaginary plate and putting it in her mouth and chewing. I was devastated. I thought we were way beyond that but it's only been 5 days since her imaginary cookie bake and I suppose not a lot of healing can happen in that time. I am so glad her kids didn't see this and I am sorry I suggested she sit up and wait. Once again, I think her meds are too strong. I will mention this to the doctor tomorrow.

PERTINENT MEDICAL NOTES
MADONNA REHABILITATION HOSPITAL

NURSING STAFF NOTE:

11:20 AM. No change in overall status. Patient arouses without difficulty, responds by head nods and shakes and occasional verbal response. Voice is very soft. Affect remains very flat. Cooperative with activities of daily living but is rather guarded in her mannerisms. Showered by herself with standby assist. Gait is slightly wobbly but did not observe patient lose balance. Toilets with standby assist. Father here this a.m. and ambulates with her in the hallways. Patient denies headache. Still naps at intervals.

Chapter 15

Monday, February 25, 2008

"Mom, I Have Always Needed You!"

MY NARRATIVE

I returned to work in Omaha today. I am a medical technologist for a large regional reference laboratory. I am Director of Professional Services and we have all our administration meetings on Monday so I decided to attend them today. Greg took Michelle to the hospital today for the ultrasound of her kidneys, liver, and gall bladder. Her liver enzymes were elevated so the doctor wanted to have these procedures to rule out other injuries.

The following notes were in her Memory Book:

PT: Rode NU-step bike 10 minutes, practiced walking over unlevel surfaces

OT: Completed multistep money management tasks, scanned bills to find information

ST: Logic puzzle, Michelle was tired but agreed to work for a bit--she was able to carryover use of strategies for completing puzzles.

OT: (afternoon schedule) Worked on list making to assist with memory and recall and daily sequencing of tasks. Michelle wrote out her schedule as follows:

Monday: Kids

Tuesday: Work, kids to Diana's

Wednesday: Work, kids to Diana's

Thursday: Work, kids to Diana's

Friday: Kids

Saturday: Kids

Sunday: Kids

Michelle then said she was feeling sick and got up and walked back to her room.

ST: (afternoon schedule) Completed a scheduling task-did fairly well, provided rationales when prompted, listened to a short news article, used note-taking with strategies to help with recall.

An ice storm moved into Nebraska as one of my colleagues and I made our way home from Omaha. The trip that usually takes 1 hour was stretching to 2 hours. We encountered black ice with cars spinning around in front of us and traffic creeping on the interstate and in town once we got to Lincoln. It was dark when I walked in the house and the phone was ringing. Greg was on the phone saying I needed to get to Madonna as soon as possible. I could hear Michelle in the background and I could tell that she was hysterical and I was frantic.

I quickly changed clothes and grabbed the food that one of my co-worker's mom had made for Greg and the kids. I have not mentioned how wonderful family and friends have been with providing food for Greg and the kids. Friends are truly incredible.

I drove slowly to the hospital and when I got there Michelle was insisting that she had to go home. She said to me: "Mom, you don't know what they do to me when you aren't here. They stick me with needles. Just go look out there and look at all the syringes by my chart. They are going to give me more shots. They are trying to drug me so I can't get up." I tried to reason with her but she was just insistent. I finally said, "Michelle, I will stay with you all night and I will go to every treatment with you. I will be with you every minute and I won't let anyone give you shots or medicine unless I know what it is. I will also call Lane (her doctor) and have him come over here and check your medication records."

This calmed her down and she finally let Greg go home to the kids. I called my husband and asked him to bring me some clothes. I was planning to be there the rest of the time she was at Madonna. I called Lane, and asked him if he could stop by Madonna and calm her down about the meds she was being given. When he heard how upset she was, he got in his car and drove over the ice to come to Madonna and sit with her. He assured her he would review all her meds with the nurses and he also reviewed her chart to make sure she had not been given anything that was not ordered. His reassurance calmed her down and she changed into her own comfy pajamas and crawled into bed to sleep.

About 9:30 she woke up and said, "Mom, I itch all over. This happens every night. I wake up and I just itch everywhere." I found some lotion in the bag Greg had brought to the hospital and I rubbed it on her arms and legs. It was a new fragrance to me--some kind of Japanese flowers-- and it smelled wonderful! I was smelling flowers again! She relaxed and said, "Thanks that helps." I asked her where she got it and she said: Oh, Greg gave it to me for Christmas but I hadn't used it yet."

I pushed her hair out of her face and off her forehead. She opened her eyes and looked at me. I said, "Michelle, it's so nice to be here with you and so nice being able to help you. You haven't needed me like this for a long time." She looked right at me and said, "Mom, I have always needed you."

I stood quietly by her bed and continued stroking her hair and soothing her forehead and she drifted off to sleep, never seeing the tears that were streaming down my face. "*Dear God, Please heal this child of mine. She has kids to raise and a husband that loves her. She needs to return to her family and the life that she loved. She does need me Lord, she needs me here with her. Help me be strong and please show me how to lead her back. Help me calm her fears. How I love this girl! Somehow let this love of mine flow into her and give her strength. Please continue healing her brain,*"

After Michelle was sleeping soundly I laid back down and tried to go to sleep. I kept going over and over the true hysteria that greeted me when I arrived at Madonna today. I just couldn't understand what had happened to make her so frightened. I couldn't sleep, so I got up and went out to the nurses' station and asked the nurses if anything had happened that would have upset her so much.

One of the nurses told me Michelle had been sleeping in the latter part of the afternoon and when she woke up, she decided to take a shower. She proceeded to go to the bathroom by herself and started getting ready for her shower. Of course, her alarm went off and a nurse assistant came in to see why she had gotten up without using her call light (which she never uses!!!). The nurse told me that there were no towels in the bathroom so the nurse assistant made Michelle get back in her net bed (without any clothes on) and zipped her in there while she went to get a towel. Michelle was very upset when the nurse assistant returned and that must have led to her melt down when Greg got there.

I was surprised to see that there was no mention of this incident in the nursing notes today as I feel certain it was the triggering event that led to her hysteria. I will be with her from now on so she doesn't suffer any more set-backs.

PERTINENT MEDICAL NOTES
MADONNA REHABILITATION HOSPITAL

SPEECH THERAPY STAFF NOTE

> 11:30 AM Therapy session focused on cognitive communication. Patient husband present for session. Patient in bed, initially refusing to participate however with encouragement, patient completed therapy task. Patient given moderate complex logic deductive reasoning puzzles. Demonstrates increased independent use of strategies shown in previous sections for recognition of complete vs. vague clues. Patient showing good accuracy initially, then demonstrates increased impulsivity and lack of attending to details as well as monitoring. Patient then ignored final three items leaving puzzle incomplete. Therapist then provided review of all items completed patient was only able to correct 1 item omitted. Patient attempted to relate activities performed in therapy for memory book, although was inaccurate and confabulated information.

Chapter 16

Tuesday, February 26, 2008

Mom and Michelle Draw Up a Contract

MY NARRATIVE

This morning, about 7:00 AM, Michelle was not allowed to get out of bed. Her blood pressure was 75/39 taken by machine, the manual (old fashioned way) was 70/40. They brought her some juice and a big glass of water and told her she had to stay in bed until her blood pressure is normal.

By 9:00 it had returned to her normal range and she had eaten breakfast and gotten dressed and was ready for her therapies. I continue to wonder if her meds are causing unusually low blood pressure. Her blood pressure is normally on the low side anyway, so it doesn't take much to make it drop.

ST: Looked at items in phonebook to compare--generated questions to ask and will complete calls at a later time.

PT: Walked to gym, rode NU step bike for 15 minutes, did standing balance exercises

OT: Worked on vision, went to cafeteria and practiced selecting foods, talked about going to HyVee Grocery for her "out of facility" activity.

PT: Walked through facility 1 lap then Michelle went back to her room.

OT: Made brownies. Michelle said they would be for the kids that night.

ST: Internet search for E-bay items.

Michelle didn't want to go to any more therapy today but there was a computer outside her room. I suggested to the Speech Therapist that she be allowed to use the computer. Michelle jumped at the chance and the therapist asked Michelle if she knew how to use E-Bay. The Therapist said she had never been able to figure it out. Michelle got right on line and found E-bay and explained that sometimes you could buy it immediately without having to bid. I was impressed! I learned something that day. The therapist wrote: "good work"

Michelle and I had a visit today from one of the psychologist's and one of the head nurses at Madonna. They told me they knew Michelle was unhappy and they thought it was slowing down her progress. Michelle told them she HATED the cage on her bed and so they agreed to take it off. She then said she would be more cooperative about her therapies. As soon as they left, she went into the bathroom and started carrying out her hair brushes, shampoo, toothbrush, etc. She placed them in the very straight line all along the end of her bed in preparation to loading them into her suitcase. I asked what she was doing and she said she was getting ready to go home. She said the people we had just met with told her she could go home now.

I told her that wasn't right. She was very angry with me and crawled in bed and said, "If I can't go home, I am going to stop taking my meds and then I will just die because I can't stand to be here any more." I was shocked!

I decided she needed to be shocked, too.

I said, "Michelle, you are not a quitter, you are a fighter. If you want to get out of here you have to fight. You can't lie around and quit on the therapies, the therapies are what will help you get home. But, you have to do more. You have to talk to your kids, you have to hold them, you have to hug them. You have not even held them since the accident.'

She looked at me and said, "I haven't?"

I responded, "No!. When you were home with your kids, you would read books to the twins and Grace is learning to read and you would hold her and listen to her read. You asked Geran about his preschool. You have to be able to be a mom to them before you can even think about going home. You have to start fighting harder. You have to decide. If you decide to fight, I will help you get home sooner. But, you have to decide if you are a fighter or a quitter."

She stayed in bed about an hour with her back to me. Her eyes were open but she was staring at the wall and I know she was plotting and planning! All of a sudden she got up and went to the phone and called Greg. She told him she was going to be going home pretty soon. She also said she wanted him to bring the kids up and bring pizza tonight. She said she wanted them to all eat in her room with her.

When she hung up, she looked at me and said, "Ok, mom, I have decided that I am going to fight, but you have to help me get out of here." I said, "OK, I will, but once you are out, you have to come back during the day for your therapies and I don't want any arguing about coming back."

Michelle: OK

Mom: OK, Michelle, I am writing a contract and you have to sign it because I am not going to have you arguing with me every day about your therapies.

Michelle: OK

Mom wrote:

I agree to work hard at my therapies 3 X per week. I want to be able to drive, cook, grocery shop, return to work, kid's swimming lessons, attend track and baseball, and hug my kids and take care of them. I will work hard to once again be Michelle

---

She signed it and we looked at each other and smiled! She had that coy little smile again, the one she gave me when she tried to leave via the emergency exits. She is definitely up to something but I was sincere in helping her because she isn't accomplishing much when she is so miserable here.

Tonight, Greg brought the kids and brought pizza just as she had requested. I covered her tray with a big towel and we had pizza and the brownies Michelle had baked that morning. Of course the kids dived into the food but they kept their distance from Michelle. They looked at her but stayed next to their dad and always asked him if they wanted more. They are not used to interacting with her any more.

Michelle finally asked Grace to bring her a book to read and soon Geran was on the bed beside her listening to Grace reading the story. Michelle had her arms around both of them and slowly the twins wanted to be on the bed with her, too. By the end of the evening, the twins had each brought her a book they wanted her to read. Michelle was able to read the books to them and she even pointed out pictures and talked about what the pictures were.

Michelle was exhausted when they left but also proud of herself for being a mom again. The goal had been set by the staff at Madonna that she had to be able to spend 1 hour with the kids but 2 1/2 hours had passed without Michelle noticing or wanting everyone to leave. She smiled more in that 2 1/2 hours than anytime since the accident.

Michelle's statement: "If I can't go home, I am going to stop taking my meds and then I will just die because I can't stand to be here any more" really bothered me all night. I know depression is a very common symptom following a TBI and this statement showed me that she was definitely showing signs of depression. This is not the type of statement the "old Michelle" would have ever uttered. She actually loved her life!

People with TBI may experience a range of psychiatric symptoms such as depression, anxiety disorders, mood disorders, personality disorders, schizophrenia, and panic disorder. These individuals are also at higher risk of suicide than the non-injured population. 57% of individuals with TBI expressed lack of social network in terms of friendship or relationship with others that may contribute to poor mental health outcome. A study by Wood and Yaracuy examined the relationship status of 131 persons with TBI and reported that 49% of the sample had divorced or separated from their partners during a 5-8 year period following the TBI. Patients suffering TBI's need mental health support as well as physical support to return to a satisfying life following their injury. [8]

Depression is the most common psychiatric symptom in TBI patients with 50% of patients experiencing depression at some time throughout their recovery. A study was reported in the International Journal of Therapy and Rehabilitation that measured the depression levels of participants in an intervention group. The group of TBI patients met

---

[8] Chan, Jeffrey; Parmenter, Trevor/ and Stancliffe. Volume 8, Issue 2, 2009. *"The Impact of Traumatic Brain Injury on the Mental Health Outcomes of Individuals and Their Family Care Givers."* Australian e-Journal for the Advancement of Mental Health Pages 2-7

weekly for 8 weeks and discussed such topics as Tiredness and Fatigue, Anxiety, and Depression. Participants completed questionnaires 3 months before the first meeting, one month before, and just before the group started. Data was again collected in the middle of the intervention and again at the end. There was a break in session for 1 1/2 months during which time data was collected every 2 weeks. The second session was also 8 weeks and covered topics such as Relationships, Memory, Habits, Planning and Goal Setting, and Health living. A questionnaire with open ended questions was given to the group near the end of the second week. Comments such as: "Yes, I understand what is wrong with me and I can adjust accordingly," and "I would have liked for something to fall back on when the meetings ended." All participants expressed an interest in continuing to meet together as a kind of "self help" group. The authors felt the patients could significantly see a reduction in depression by participating in a peer group and felt more studies should be done to evaluate the effectiveness of peer group sessions following TBI. [9]

I remembered the discussions with the staff about a Brain Injury Group that met in Lincoln. I made a note to myself to find out more about them and make sure Michelle made contact with them when she was ready to reach out to other TBI victims for support.

PERTINENT MEDICAL NOTES
MADONNA REHABILITATION HOSPITAL

CARE PLAN PROGRESS REPORT
1. Changes in goals or anticipated length of stay: Yes. To continue to evaluate, may need to extend stay post 3-1-08 decreased safety awareness.
2. Discharge plan/aftercare services: Home with family and outpatient therapy, possibly rehab day program.
3. Patient and or family input: Family including husband and parents supportive of ongoing rehab plan.
4. Barriers: Wants to leave, impulsive, decreased insight into deficits, agitated, will be on locked unit for safety when needed, bland effect, not always wanting to participate, fatigues easily.
5. Changes in treatment plan: Independent with transfers, discontinue net bed, discontinue side pads X increase Celexa to 20 mg on 2/27/08.
6. Current status: Not remembering things day to day, won't use memory log. Oriented to date and time, can do structured familiar tasks. Participates but when distracted and impulsive can't remain on task. Can do simple math, moderate money management skills, ambulates with standby assistance, fatigues easily, decreased endurance. Requires standby assist with activities of daily living.

---

[9] Forman CM, Vasey, PA Lincoln, NB (2006) *"Effectiveness of an adjustment group for brain injury patients: A pilot evaluation."* International Journal of Therapy & Rehabilitation (13)5 223-228

Chapter 17

Wednesday, February 27, 2008

"I'll Have 1/2 lb of Summer Sausage Cut in 1/8 Inch Thick slices."

MY NARRATIVE

Wednesday morning the doctor came in and said he understood Michelle wanted to go home. Once more, she had lined up her cosmetics on the end of the bed in preparation for packing them up. He told her she had to finish her therapies that day, including one outside Madonna in the city. We reviewed the meds she would need and he made me promise she would have 24/7 adult supervision and that could not include also watching the children. We had to have someone for the kids and someone for her. I agreed that we could do this.

I showed him the contract Michelle had made with me and he was happy we had done that and that she had signed it. I also told him about the evening she had spent with the kids. He reviewed her meds with me and explained why she needed each one.

As soon as he was out of the door, Michelle looked at me and said: "Mom, I don't trust him, I don't think you should either."

Mom: "Why don't you trust him, Michelle? He's the doctor that has worked so hard to get your meds adjusted so you aren't so tired all the time. He has worked carefully to make sure your therapies are matched to what you need. I can't believe you don't trust HIM?"

Michelle: "I just don't and I don't think you should either. I think he just wants to keep me here longer to make more money!"

Mom: "Michelle, that doesn't make any sense. He's on salary here, he gets paid the same whether you are here or not, he just wants to see you healed and ready to return to your life."

Michelle: "Well, I don't trust him."

Mom: "Who do you trust?"

Michelle: "I trust you and Greg."

Mom: "How about Dad?"

Michelle: "Oh, yes, I trust Dad, too?

Mom: "Good, well you know one of us will always be with you here so you can relax and focus on your therapies and know that someone you trust is with you all the time."

Her therapies today:

ST: Computer task, accessed health clubs and compared costs. She does well with computer tasks and likes doing them.

PT: Walked in halls, didn't want to do barbells or machines in GYM

OT: Outing to HyVee (more about this later)

PT: To Gym and back, Rode NU-step bike 15 minutes 3 times. Did Balance exercises.

ST: Learned a new game--RACKO--did well!

Her trip to HyVee was memorable. We used my car since the Madonna car had already been spoken for. The Occupational Therapist sat in the back seat and asked Michelle where she usually shopped. She replied at HyVee, so off we went. On the way from Madonna to the car, Michelle walked right out into the parking lot without looking for cars or anything--just headed straight for my car. She was able to give good directions on how to get to the grocery store. Once we parked in the parking lot, she again just jumped out of the car and started walking through the parking lot not even looking for cars.

One of the Occupational Therapist used the term "agnosia" for Michelle's lapses in memory when trying to do old familiar tasks. We observed it in the kitchen mixing things to bake. I saw it when she was sitting waiting for her food. The OT told me she again displayed it while making brownies just yesterday. The "lack of awareness" thing is still with her.. She truly does not realize that she doesn't have a scissors in her hand or that she isn't measuring water. I see it again as we walk through the parking lot, she had no awareness of traffic moving around her. She just pushes along like she is the only person in the parking lot.

Once inside, she grabbed a shopping cart and we were off! She knew where things were in this store, but paid no attention to other shoppers. She careened in and around other shoppers but she did manage to avoid them and had no collisions! I thought the best thing she did was stop at the deli and order a specific brand of summer sausage and said she wanted 1/2 lb and told him exactly how she wanted it sliced.

When we got to the check-out line Michelle looked at me and said, "Mom, I can't go through the check out line. I need to put all this back! You need to help me put it all back!" She looked panicked!

I asked her why she couldn't go through the check-out line.

She looked at me incredulously and said, "Well, Mom, I don't have any money!"

I breathed a sigh of relief as I had thought maybe she was afraid to be in line with other people. Silly me! She realized she hadn't brought any money along! I quickly reassured her that if these were things we needed at her house, I could buy them and she could just pay me back sometime. That brought a smile of relief to her face and we checked out and returned to our car.

The Occupational Therapist had told her to make a list before we left and she did, but she never got it out of her pocket. Michelle also went up and down every aisle. The OT asked me if this was how she always shopped and I honestly didn't know. I had never shopped for groceries with my daughter! I called Greg and he said, "Oh, yeah, she goes up and down every aisle and she never makes a list." so this was normal for her. After we got back to the car, the OT had her pull out her list and she had gotten everything on it, plus a few extras.

On the way back to Madonna, the OT said Michelle had to direct us to drive a different route than the one we took to get to HyVee and Michelle did this with no problems. She passed her goals for OT and surpassed them for PT so she was allowed to go home. She had done it! She is a fighter, just as I knew she was!

Michelle once again lined up her cosmetics on the bed and this time we packed them up in the little suitcase Greg had brought for her. Greg picked her up about 6:30 PM and after signing all the discharge papers, she was on her way home! Once she got there, she was so tired she went to bed almost immediately!

PERTINENT MEDICAL NOTES
MADONNA REHABILITATION HOSPITAL

PLANNED DISCHARGE GOAL/DATE:

This patient was admitted to Madonna Rehabilitation Hospital Acute Rehab unit on 2/15/08. Patient was a transfer from BryanLGH West. Patient was in a motor vehicle accident on February 11, 2008. She suffered a complicated mild traumatic brain injury from this accident and now has been transferred to an Acute Rehab level of care. The team has estimated she will need an approximate two week length of stay making her approximate discharge date March 1, 2008.

GOALS:

1. Patient will complete self-care's independently with adaptive equipment as needed. (goal not met)
2. Patient will complete slight homemaking, activities independently. (goal not met)
3. Patient will require standby assist with childcare activities for one hour. (goal met)
4. Patient will demonstrate increased muscle strength by 10 pounds for independence with meal prep. (goal met)
5. Patient will perform bed mobility independently. (goal met)
6. Patient will perform functional transfers independently. (goal met)
7. Patient will be able to ambulate greater than 1000 feet without adaptive device independently. (goal not met)
8. Patient will have increased BERG space balance score of greater than 45 out of 56. (goal met)
9. Patient will be able to ascend/descend a flight of stairs with a handrail independently. (goal met)
10. Patient will demonstrate characteristics of a Rancho Los Amigos level VIII. (goal not met)

REASONS FOR CONTINUED STAY/CURRENT STATUS:

Patient discharged home with family several day sooner than anticipated. The patient met 6 out of 10 of her long-term goals while in acute rehab. The patient became increasingly angry about being on an inpatient unit, and was continuing to perseverate on going home. Family decided to go ahead and take the patient home and provide 24 hour supervision and follow-up in our rehab day program as an outpatient.

Speech therapy reported no formal discharge was completed, however the discharge information was completed using recent performances. They are recommending continued speech therapy for cognitive communication and executive functions. Patient is currently at a Rancho Los Amigos level VII, demonstrates decreased insight and awareness into deficits.

Occupational therapy reported patient required standby assist with self-cares and home management tasks secondary to decreased cognition, decreased safety awareness and sequencing.

Physical therapy reported the patient was independent with transfers, independent with bed mobility, ambulates independently 1000+ feet without gait deviations and no adaptive device. Needs supervision in community due to cognitive deficits. Patient was independent with ascending/descending 12 steps with a handrail. Patient scored 56 out of 56 on the Berg balance test.

Recommendations were to continue with occupational, physical, and speech therapy in our rehab day program.

Chapter 18

Thursday, February 28, 2008

"Mom, I'm So Glad You're Back."

MY NARRATIVE

    Michelle is home and had a good night's sleep. She does not have to start outpatient therapies until next Monday so she has a few days to acclimate to being home. We are going to keep the kids on their same schedule so Grace went to school and Geran, Aidan, and Alysen went to Diana's. She says it feels surreal to be home, she can't believe what happened to her and she keeps hoping she will wake up from the dream. She rode with me to take the kids to Diana's then we came home and she slept. She does not have a good appetite so her meals are quick and light.

    In the afternoon, we had a doctor's appointment with her neurosurgeon. He needed to check her "probe" hole and see how she is doing. The office is hard to find, tucked away in one of the wings of the Doctor's Office Building that is connected to BryanLGH where Michelle had been taken after the accident. We did make it by 3:00 but when we opened the door of the office, my heart sunk! The waiting room was full and I have a bad feeling about how this was going to go. Memories of the Eye Doctor exam are flooding my brain with warning signs.

Within 10 minutes, Michelle is ready to leave.

Michelle: "Mom, I was supposed to see him at 3:00. We shouldn't have to sit around here and wait. You have things to do and you're taking time off work to take me to the appointment. Let's just leave."

Mom: "Michelle, let me check with the receptionist and see how long it will be. I'm sure you are next to be called." (I am not at all sure but I am hoping.)

Mom: (To receptionist) "Can you tell me how much longer it will be before Michelle is called?"

Receptionist: "No, we are short nurses today so we are running a little behind."

Mom: "Could you at least put us in a room? My daughter has ah - ah - -" - (here I am stumbling around for the words that are so hard for me to say)- - - "she has a traumatic brain injury and she has just been released from Madonna Rehab Hospital. She doesn't understand the concept of time and waiting yet. She is very restless and wants to leave."

Receptionist: "Well, I could talk to one of the nurses, if I can even catch one of them, but it is just going to be a wait today since we are short staffed. One of our nurses is out sick today." (Giggles and shrugs shoulders.)

Mom (To Michelle) "Well, Michelle, one of their nurses is sick today so they are running a little behind.

Michelle: "Well, let's just go. We can come back some other time. Or, I don't even need to see this guy. I don't know who he is, I don't even know if he has ever seen me. Let's just go."

Mom: "Well, since I went up and asked, I think we can wait another 5 minutes. I bet they'll have a room for you then."

10 minutes later. Michelle: "Mom, let's just go. This is ridiculous. You need to get back to work and I need to get the kids home from Diana's. Let's just go."

Mom: "Let me check one more time and see how close you are."

Mom: (To receptionist) "I can't keep her here anymore. Do you have a room for us? I am sure if we just got her in a room, she would be able to wait a little longer."

Receptionist: (Sighs) "Let me see what I can do." (Returns) "OK, someone's going to call you back in just a few minutes."

Mom: "Thank you. I really do appreciate it."

Mom (To Michelle) "They are going to call us next, our room is ready."

We still wait 5 minutes but we do get called back and escorted to an exam room. It is still another 15 minutes before the doctor comes but there are lots of things to look at in the room. The doctor came in and asked Michelle how she was doing. Her reply surprised and pleased me. She said, "I'm sorry I was such a pain in the waiting room. I just can't stand to sit around and not be doing something." I was happy she recognized that she had been a pain!

The doctor was very helpful and showed us MRI's of her brain. He said she had had blood in her spinal fluid when they brought her in but the main damage had been in the frontal lobe and he expected her to make a full recovery. He said her skull from the hole they had made for the probe in her brain that monitored her pressure in the brain was healing nicely and he needed to see her again in a month to make sure the healing was completed.

After we left his office we stopped and got hot chai tea as the weather is still very cold. Then I stopped at an office supply store to buy a folding file for Greg. He is already getting so many bills and insurance forms, I offered to get him something to keep them all separated.

Greg and Michelle had HMO insurance and their maximum out-of-pocket expenses were $4,000 per year. I'm sure that amount was consumed during the emergency room and intensive care services the first day. Greg and Michelle also had a medical insurance rider along with their car insurance so this should not be a financial burden for the family. It is just a matter of getting all the papers filed with the right insurer!

I parked so Michelle could see me in the store and she agreed to wait in the car since it was so cold. I was back in less than 5 minutes and she said: "Mom, I'm so glad you're back. I don't know what's wrong with me but whenever anyone leaves me, I feel like they are never coming back. Even when I could see you in the store, I was worried that you wouldn't come back to me: Why do I feel this way?" I told her it was her "accident brain" and that pretty soon she would have her "old, good brain" back and then she wouldn't have those feelings any more. She didn't look convinced!

She still has not cried! But, her mind is working now and asking questions and I think she is struggling to make sense of it all. I am hoping that these 4 days at home will give her a chance to glimpse her old life in familiar surroundings. Maybe this will provide her brain with some additional cues so it is challenged to quickly repair and reroute the pathways, around the damaged areas and reconnect to her healthy brain cells.

I mentioned the financial aspects of this accident. Michelle and Greg are fortunate to have insurance in place to cover all her acute and rehabilitation needs. After a TBI, the financial impact should be one of the first things that is evaluated. Families that are faced with helping a child or spouse or a parent with recovery from a TBI face many obstacles on the road to normalcy. One issue faced by all families is the financial obligations that are part of a successful outcome.

The family should make sure they are familiar with the patient's insurance coverage so that there are no surprises as medical care and rehabilitation progress. If possible, ask one member of the family to be responsible for monitoring bills as they come in and working with the insurance company. A good suggestion is to ask the insurance company to assign a case manager at the insurance company to form a collaborative relationship early on. If rehabilitation services are not provided by the insurance company, investigate long-term coverage from government programs such as Social Security, Medicare, and Medicaid. If the patient's insurance does not cover long term rehabilitation services, information and forms from the government should be acquired and filled out because the application and approval takes months. [10]

In addition to Insurance coverage, any legal issues should be addressed as soon as possible. Again, this may be the job for one member of the family or a family friend that has time to pursue finding an experienced attorney. If liability issues are one of the concerns, an attorney familiar with head injuries should be contacted. The state Bar Association or the state Brain Injury Association should be able to provide a list of names of attorneys with experience handling cases involving brain injuries. The sooner an attorney is involved, the easier it will be for the family to make informed decisions regarding rehabilitation and home care. An attorney's help may also be needed for power of attorney documents or health care directives. [11]

There are statistics regarding the average cost of medical services associated with TBI. Total estimated annual costs for the U.S. based on a rate of 2% of the population, related to traumatic brain injury are estimated at $60 billion. This includes severe, moderate, and mild brain injury. This total cost estimate includes both fatal and nonfatal injuries and medical costs and productivity losses. Using national research and the estimated 2% cited above, the total estimated brain injury costs for Nebraska in 2009 was $413,513,208.

---

10 *"Resources for People with Brain Injury and Their Families."* TBI National Resource Center, Virginia Commonwealth University, Neuropsychology and Rehabilitations Psychology Division, Department of Physical Medicine and Rehabilitation, Retrieved on January 9, 2014 from www.tbirc.com/resources-for-people-with-brain-injury-and-their-families.

11 *"Resources for People with Brain Injury and Their Families."* TBI National Resource Center, Virginia Commonwealth University, Neuropsychology and Rehabilitations Psychology Division, Department of Physical Medicine and Rehabilitation, Retrieved on January 9, 2014 from www.tbirc.com/resources-for-people-with-brain-injury-and-their-families.

It is estimated that the lifetime costs for:

> Mild brain injury: $85,000
> Moderate brain injury: $941,000
> Severe brain injury: $3 million [12]

In July 2012, The Mayo Clinic, Olmsted Medical Center, and their hospital affiliates published a study they had done regarding the treatment costs of TBI. They matched accident victims that suffered TBI's with accident victims with the same physical injuries but without a TBI. They studied these paired patients for 6 years. They concluded that patients with TBI's classified as **"possible"** incurred a total cost of $2,178,625 which was 43% higher than the $1,522,935 spent for cases classified as **"probable"** and 14% higher that the $1,916,172 spent on cases classified as **"definite"** TBI's. They theorized that one reason for the higher cost is <u>lack of early diagnosis</u> with some patients not being diagnosed as "possible" one year post injury. They suggest that early diagnosis would lead to earlier treatment. [13]

Early diagnosis is critical to positive outcomes and long term recovery. If you have a child or loved one that has been unconscious, insist that they are tested by knowledgeable staff and that they have the diagnostic tests necessary to rule out a traumatic brain injury.

Michelle and Greg were fortunate to have Michelle's head injury diagnosed immediately. They were also fortunate to have in place the necessary insurance to cover the costs of Michelle's recovery. However, Greg spent countless hours matching EOB (Explanation of Benefits) forms to Invoices from the acute hospital, the rehab hospital and the many physicians that treated Michelle during her acute, rehab, and out-patient phases of her TBI. Handling the finances associated with TBI is a formidable challenge.

---

12 *"Nebraska TBI needs and Resources Assessment Survey."* Page 1. Retrieved on November 14, 2013 from www.biane.org/what/nebraska.html

13 Leibson CL, Brown AW, Long KH, Ransom JE, Mandrekar J, Osler TM, Malec MF: July 20, 2012 *"Medical Care Costs Associated with Traumatic Brain Injury over the Full Spectrum of Disease: A Controlled Population-Based Study."* July 20, 2012 Journal of Neurotrauma, 29: 2038-2049

Chapter 19

Friday, February 29, 2008

The Fog is Lifting

MY NARRATIVE

    Michelle has enjoyed being home and interacting once again with her children. She keeps mentioning how "weird" she feels--like she is in a dream and she will wake up and none of this ever happened. Sometimes she calls it a nightmare. She said she just feels disconnected and things are not in sync. She also announced she is no longer going to blow-dry her hair. It is much too noisy and the sound hurts her head! Maybe it is time for a shorter hair cut!

    This morning, Katie, a college friend came to see Michelle. Katie is another sorority sister that was actually her sorority baby! Michelle was not able to carry on much of a conversation with her and I was surprised. I finally had them bundle up and take a little walk outside as Katie had never seen Michelle's house and the acreage and I thought Michelle might be able to tell her a little about it.

Greg proposed to Michelle on this acreage on Christmas Eve. He had bought the acreage and driven her out there and parked in the middle of it and asked her to marry him. He is a project manager for a Restoration company and through his work has learned many parts of the construction trade. He oversaw the building of their home and did lots of the work himself. It is a beautiful home on a beautiful acreage complete with a little pond in front of the home. He and Michelle have worked hard to create a real peaceful and safe setting for their family. I think being back on their land will help Michelle begin to reconnect again as this land is such a part of their history together.

Katie stayed with the twins and started making lunch and Michelle and I went to pick up Geran from preschool. Michelle didn't want to go in with me to get him, she just wanted to stay in the car and be there when he came out. She had a big smile on her face when Geran and I walked out of "Wee Wisdom" and toward our car. Geran was thrilled to see his mom waiting for him.

This afternoon, Michelle got up from her nap and walked into the twin's bedroom while they were sleeping. She did this about 4 times. I was afraid she would wake them up. She said she just needed to check on them and make sure they were still in their beds.

She went back to her room and then returned and said,: "I have just lost 3 weeks of my life, haven't I. About 10 minutes later she walked back out and said, "Weren't you and dad supposed to be in Palm Desert?" I was so surprised. We had not ever mentioned that we cut short our vacation to come home. I asked her if she had that written on her calendar and she said, "No, I just somehow remembered that you were supposed to be there." This is a good sign! The brain is making new pathways and she is beginning to reconnect with her old memories.

She wanted to see the cards she had gotten. I showed her the pictures of the flowers and what each person had written. She said, "Mom, how will I ever thank them all!" Yes, her brain is starting to find itself again!

The twins woke up and crawled up on their chairs in the kitchen and began coloring. Michelle became more animated and interacted with them more naturally. I asked her if she felt more connected and she said, "Yes, I do, I really do!" They have lots of questions about the accident and why she hit the tree. I keep reminding them that mommy's brain was hurt and it needs rest. It hurts her head when they make too much noise and to help mommy's brain get better, Mommy needs to take naps. They look at me and try to take it in but, pretty much, they think mom is home and things are back to normal.

I believe the fog is lifting. I am anxious to see how the weekend goes. She will have lots more company so things will be more of a challenge. People are so glad to see her up and around and most have no idea about her frustrations over being at Madonna and her "phantom actions" throughout her stay there. For some reason neither Greg nor I have mentioned these in our daily notes on Care Pages. Am I still in denial about the reality of this accident? I don't know, but I guess I probably am still in Stage 1 myself!

    I am glad we brought Michelle home from Madonna a few days early. I think here, in her own home, she can begin to piece together the parts of her life that have been torn apart. I think she needed to be here to speed up the healing. The real test will come Monday when it is time to return to Madonna for outpatient therapy. I have my contract close at hand in case she tries to talk us out of going back.

Chapter 20
Saturday and Sunday March 1 & 2, 2008
Today Michelle Cried!

MY NARRATIVE:

Greg's family came Saturday and stayed with the family. The weather was nice and Michelle walked out to the mailbox several times. Of course, the kids went with her to "help Mommy!" Greg reported that she was still somewhat disconnected from them but she watched Geran play baseball outside with Daddy and Grandpa Jerry and she spent a little time on the playground set in the back yard. In the evening they all piled into her new Suburban and went and got pizza!

Sunday was a break-through day. Michelle cried!! My daughter, Melissa, offered to stay with the family on Sunday so Larry and I could have a full weekend at home to catch up on our household tasks. It was also good to have some down time to renew and refresh ourselves. Melissa reported that Michelle had many tears throughout the day. She kept asking, "How could this happen? Why to me, Why to us? Why are you here doing all the things I should be doing? Why can't I take care of my own kids?

This is a good thing and I am relieved that she finally is beginning to understand! I think this is a sign that she is really healing and beginning to come back to us. She is beginning to live back in her "old, good brain" again. She had lots of family visiting so that just impressed upon her even more how serious the accident had been.

A neighbor brought the family a great dinner and cookies. People want to help and are finding ways to do so.

On Michelle's Care Page, Greg wrote tonight, "Michelle is in the room next to my office playing a game with the kids . . . and yelling at them for being so crazy. Things are slowly getting back to normal!"

Chapter 21

Week 1 of Outpatient Therapy

March 3-March 9, 2008

"Mom, You Don't Know How Comforting It Is To Remember Yesterday!"

MY NARRATIVE

    Michelle and I started Out-Patient Therapy at Madonna Rehabilitation's Day Program. Last Monday I promised her she would not be alone for any treatments. Either Larry or Greg or I will be with her for all her therapies. I do not want any of her fears to keep her from progressing through all her therapies so one of us is still accompanying her to every treatment. I picked her up at 7:30 at her home. I had our contract in my purse in case there were any problems but she came right out to the car with me. I think she realizes that she needs this therapy. The weekend opened her eyes to what had really happened to her.

    We arrived at 8:00 AM and Michelle was handed her schedule for the day. She was also assigned a locker where she could hang her coat and leave her purse or other personal articles.

Michelle met with an APRN that performed another history and physical on her. She reported that Michelle's physical injuries were almost completely healed. She reviewed meds with Michelle and asked her in detail about Michelle's ability to sleep. So far, this has not been a problem for Michelle. The nurse stressed with her that if she had any trouble sleeping, they would give her some sleeping meds because she really needed to sleep well during the night to give her brain a chance to heal over the long hours of the night.

Sleep-Wake Cycle Disturbance is prevalent in TBI patients and this inability to sleep soundly and deeply each night could contribute to the patient's confusion, agitation, and poor memory. Patients are sometimes diagnosed or referred for mental health counseling without first verifying the patient is sleeping well each night.[14]

She had sessions with Physical Therapy, Occupational Therapy, Speech Therapy and a meeting with the Social Worker. In Physical Therapy, it was decided that they did not need to see her anymore. They felt she was much improved with her balance and was able to perform all the activities that she needed to pass out of Physical Therapy so that's one set of sessions we don't have to do each day.

She met with a Social Worker for the first time and that was a very good meeting.. I sat with Michelle and the Social Worker and she visited with us about the brain and how it worked and how it would help Michelle recover.

She talked about the brain having millions of cells that were never used and when one cell is damaged another cell immediately tries to learn that other cell's activity. She also told us that when blood encounters a brain cell, that the brain cell is killed and since Michelle had blood in her spinal fluid I believe this explains the numerous contusions that they talked about throughout her brain. We also learned that her brain would round up these damaged cells and slowly move them out of the brain. The social worker said they would slowly turn into an almost gelatin like material and dissolve and be moved out of the brain by the movement of the spinal fluid and cells that were available would take their place and learn the job of the old cells.

She asked Michelle about taking drugs or smoking cigarettes and Michelle told her that she had done neither of these so she assured Michelle that her brain was quite vital and quite capable of renewing itself and that she was fortunate that she had never damaged any of her cells by smoking or by taking drugs.

I asked why they started her therapy at Madonna with such difficult things the first day. Her answer was very enlightening. She said if they started with, "What is 2 + 2?"

---

14 Weiner, W J, Porter N, Shin R, Lewis S L. (2010) Neurology for the Non-neurologist: Philadephia, PA; Lippincott; Page 335

the brain would probably know that answer right away so it would relax and think it was back to normal. The brain has to be challenged and has to realize that it used to be able to do complicated things so it immediately goes about looking for new cells to train to perform these more difficult tasks. I found this fascinating. She said even cells that used to be controlling something like the cells a baby used when crawling--these cells realize that they don't need to do crawling anymore and they can be trained to learn something new. Madonna has done extensive research on the functioning of the brain and I was glad to hear that the brain keeps healing even up to 5 years or longer post accident.

These were exhausting days for Michelle but she was able to complete the tasks that the therapists had for her. We live close to Madonna so we came home for lunch and that gave her a chance to have a little power nap after lunch was over. We were always finished by 3 o'clock and she was able to take a nice long nap before we went to pick up the twins at Diana's and meet Geran and Grace and papa all at their home.

Michelle's days as an outpatient were about the same throughout the first week. She reported each morning. We came home for lunch, and she returned each afternoon. On Wednesday, while we were at home for lunch and a little nap for Michelle, I went downstairs in our home to make some phone calls. I thought she could sleep better if she didn't hear me on the phone. When I had finished my calls, I came back up and asked her if she had slept much and she said, "No, I wasn't all that tired." However, later, I would learn more about her lunch time "nap" and why she said she "wasn't all that tired."

She was in one of her Occupational Therapy sessions. She was involved in a leather stitching project and I stepped out to go to the bathroom. On my way back, I overhead a conversation between Michelle and her Therapist.

Therapist: "Michelle, why are you always looking at the clock."

Michelle: "I'm not sure, but I know I have to look for the clock, I always want to know what time it is."

Therapist: "But you have been looking at it almost all the time since your mom left."

Michelle: "I know, but I'm always afraid she won't come back and I guess if I watch the clock it helps me focus on time and not worry so much. I guess I can't explain it any better, I just need to be able to see a clock. Today, when we were home for lunch, mom went downstairs to make some phone calls and I couldn't sleep. I just kept looking at the clock. I don't know why but I was afraid that she wouldn't come back upstairs."

Therapist: "Oh, You can stop worrying now, here's your mom. Let's finish this project".

Michelle: "You know, I really don't ever sew anything, so I don't know why I have to do this!!!"

Thursday, when we were home for lunch, Michelle was standing at the sink rinsing off her lunch plate and she looked at me and said, "Mom, you don't know how comforting it is to remember yesterday." I couldn't believe what I just heard! I said, "Michelle, haven't you been remembering the days." She said, "Since Sunday, I have been remembering more and more and today I can remember all of yesterday. It is such a good feeling to remember what I talked about with people yesterday."

I admit this shocked me about as much as anything else that has happened. In the rehab center she recognized the therapists when they came to get her. She was able to answer some of the questions about previous treatments but in reality, she didn't remember the prior day's activities. But she was able to find her way all over that building. Somehow her brain had made of map of the hallways and stairs at Madonna but she couldn't remember what she did when she got where she was headed. Very Interesting! That is why she was so surprised when I told her she hadn't hugged her kids or held them or read to them. She really couldn't remember her life from one day to the next. It is interesting to me that she was unable to verbalize to us that she didn't remember things from the day before. Her "accident brain" was not telling her that she should be able to remember things from the day before.

This explains so many things regarding her agitation while at Madonna. She really was frightened that things happened to her that she couldn't remember and she needed us with her for reassurance that the day before had been okay. She needed us to tell her that we had been there and no one had given her any shots! That is also why the therapists wanted her to use her memory book. If we had read her memory book to her every day, that might have helped her remember things from the day before. If I could go back and get a "redo" on her stay at Madonna, I would definitely have read her Monday activities and visitors to her first thing Tuesday morning, her Tuesday activities and visitors first thing Wednesday morning and so on throughout the week. We would also have found a way to have someone she trusted with her all the time.

There is a name for what Michelle just described--not being able to remember things from one day to the next. It is called Post Traumatic Amnesia.

Post-Traumatic Amnesia (PTA) is a state of confusion that often appears after a Traumatic Brain Injury. The affected patient may not remember his/her name, the date, or events that happen following the injury. While PTA is in effect, the patient cannot store any new memories. The duration of amnesia and confusion is one of the best predictors of outcomes following TBI. PTA that lasts 1-7 days is ranked severe. PTA lasting 1-4 weeks it very severe, PTA lasting longer than 4 weeks is extremely severe according to Russel, Jennett and Teasdle in "Assessment of post-traumatic amnesia after severe closed head injury". [15]

Michelle's PTA lasted 3 weeks and 3 days. The above scale ranks her head injury as very severe. Hers has been ranked mild, mild complicated, moderate, and a few other descriptions throughout her hospitalization and rehabilitation. I am just thrilled that the PTA is over and that she realizes what a gift the return of her memory is.

Monday, this week, when we were at Michelle and Greg's, a neighbor, Kelly, came over to tell Michelle and Greg that many people had been asking what they could do to help. Neighbors, friends, mom's from Grace's classroom, and mom's from Geran's pre-school all were asking what they could do to help. Kelly had decided to take it upon herself to organize all these helpers for meals for the family. She had a schedule for meals Monday through Friday for 6 weeks! What a wonderful help that was for Greg and for Larry and I. Each evening someone would ring the doorbell and walk in with food for the family. It was quite remarkable and I learned from this that when people say they want to help, you should let someone else be in charge and organize a way for them to help that will truly fill a void during a crises. None of us had time to cook while looking after the children and running back and forth with Michelle so this was truly a gift that kept on giving.

Kelly also agreed to pick up Grace from school each Monday since her daughters attended the same school. Again, this helped us so much because we no longer had to wake the twins up from their nap to go pick up Grace after school. We are learning to ask for help when people offer. Our experience has been that people do really want to help, you just have to let them know what would help you the most.

On March 03, 2008 Greg wrote the following on Michelle's CarePage.

"Today marks three weeks since the accident. Three weeks this evening Michelle was in critical condition at Bryan hospital and in very good hands. Without the staff at Bryan – West, she would not be where she is today.

Today Michelle started outpatient at Madonna Rehabilitation. She did very good. Michelle aced the physical parts of her tests and will continue with the psychological and mental rehab for the next few weeks. (Thank you Madonna staff for letting Michelle come back. She was a little hard to get along with for couple of days there, but she was not herself. Michelle wants to thank you all at Madonna who helped her during her stay.)

Let's go back to Saturday, 1 March. Michelle took advantage of the 60° plus weather

---

[15] McMillian T M, Jongen, E L M M, Greenwood RJ. (1996) *"Assessment of post-traumatic amnesia after severe closed head injury: retrospective or prospective*? Journal of Neurology, Neurosurgery, and Psychiatry. Pages 422-427

and walked to the mailbox and back a couple of times. Michelle also spent a little time on the Fort/play set in the backyard with the kids. My parents spent the day and helped with the kids. Thanks mom and dad! Michelle still was a little "dreamy" and disconnected from us. She watched Geran play baseball outside with grandpa and daddy. At the end of the day we all went for a ride in her new Suburban and picked up pizza!

Sunday was a big day for Michelle. Michelle broke down in the morning sobbing, and for most of the day went in and out of this mood because she felt it was all a dream. (This marks the first emotions that Michelle's shown since the accident.) She ask why? How? How could this happen? Why are you doing all the things I'm supposed to be doing? Why can't I take care of my kids? This all means she is healing and coming back to us. We had family visiting throughout the day, and this helped her realize what happened – and she is special to us. I really feel the support and prayers from all of you made a huge difference. She keeps telling me she will thank you all, she just doesn't know how. Our neighbor Kelly just brought over a great dinner and cookies. We want to thank all reading for the food and I need to thank you all for the 10 pounds I gained. We have so much food, I just eat at night after the kids go to bed. Thanks a lot!"

In closing for tonight, Michelle is in the room next to my office playing a game with the kids... And yelling at them for being so crazy. Things are slowly getting back to normal.

PERTINENT MEDICAL NOTES
MADONNA REHABILITATION DAY PROGRAM

INTERDISCIPLINARY TREATMENT PLAN:

SHORT-TERM GOALS: Will be independent in the home and with family roles.
1. Will be independent with medicine management. Goal set 3/6/08
2. Will be independent with money management. Goal set 3/6/08
3. Plan and follow through with daily plan using external communication device with standby assist. Goal set 3/8/08
4. Will be able to demonstrate 3 energy conservation techniques throughout the day with frequent cues. Goal set 3/6/08
5. Will be able to self monitor fatigue level during functional activities using strategies with frequent cues. Goal set
6. Will plan birthday party for daughter with minimal assist. Goal set 3/6/08

LONG-TERM GOALS: Will return to community activities independently.
1. Will complete pre-driving activities at 80% success goal set 3/6/08.
2. Will plan an outing at standby assist. Goal set 3/6/08
3. Will implement outing at standby assist. Goal set 3/6/08.
4. Will state three barriers and solutions to return to work with occasional cues. Goal Set 3/6/08
5. Will meet at designated therapy locations at 80%. Goal set 3/6/08.

Chapter 22

Week 2 of Outpatient Therapy

March 10-March 16, 2008

"Well, Mom, Did I Pass Brownies 101?"

MY NARRATIVE

    This week was pretty much like the last. Michelle had therapies every day but she is getting stronger and more confident. She knows her way around all the departments and around the facility and can easily get where she needs to go for her various therapies.

    Things are also falling into a routine for us. Larry was with her Monday at Madonna and I went to Omaha for the first time in 2 weeks. I was with her Tuesday, Wednesday and Thursday and Larry went with her Friday.

    At Michelle and Greg's home, we continue to receive meals during the week and my P.E.O. group has picked up meals on Saturday evening. Pizza is a Sunday night tradition for our family and this has continued for Michelle and Greg so evening meals for the week are taken care of. There is usually food left over each evening so we certainly are not spending much time in the kitchen.

    One day this weekend, Michelle wanted to make brownies. I had told her about her baking experience at Madonna and said I had to supervise each step including the pan in and out of the oven. She had no problem with any of the steps and when the brownies were sitting on the cabinet and cooling off she looked at me with her coy little smile and said, "Well, Mom, did I pass Brownies 101." We both laughed and I silently gave thanks to God that he used this brownie baking to show me her brain is healing and she's able to begin to resume more of her old life activities or "Activities of Daily Living " as the therapists call it. There has not been one incident of the "phantom motions" since Michelle got her day-to-day memory back. I think "agnosia" is finally gone from our vocabulary!

Larry is a member of the Shrine Club here in Lincoln and every year the Lincoln Shrine brings a circus to Lincoln. Attending the Shrine Circus has been an annual event for Michelle and Greg and their kids. The Shrine Circus was this week and we already had gotten tickets for the family. Michelle wanted to go with the kids but I was nervous. There is loud music, strobe lights, loud announcers, and even a motorcycle event inside a cage that is very loud. I was sure the noise and lights would be too much for her.

She insisted that she could handle it but I wasn't convinced so I drove a separate car down to the circus so I could leave with her if everything was too much to handle. To my surprise, she stayed through the whole thing. I know it was hard on her and she had a terrible headache when it was over but she wouldn't leave. She told me, "No, mom, I want the kids to enjoy this and I don't want them to worry about me if I leave, so I'm staying." This was all in her "mom's in charge" voice. They did enjoy it and even stayed a little while afterwards to ride the elephant. I have to say this was one event that I didn't think she would be able to handle. I know it was hard for her, but she was determined to see it through. She is definitely getting stronger.

PERTINENT MEDICAL NOTES

MADONNA REHABILITATION DAY PROGRAM

OUTPATIENT CLINIC NOTE ON: S., MICHELLE M.

DATE OF SERVICE: 03/10/2008

Session sign-in time was 10:40 AM, Session sign-out time was 11:00 AM. Please note that greater than 50% of today's 20 minute session was spent in counseling and coordination of care with the patient and her father.

1. Apparently patient has been doing well at home. She is monitoring her fatigue level. She has been taking naps as needed and she is been going to bed early, trying to limit the amount of activity she does and the amount of work she does around the house. She is doing a good job of monitoring that.

2. Patient has not had any significant tearful episodes, so they did not go up on the Celexa that was recommended as a possibility last week. Therefore, she currently remains on the 20 mg of Celexa.

3. Team states she is doing well and participating in therapies, making good progress. They don't have any concerns at this time. So I'm not going to make any therapy changes.

Chapter 23

Week 3 of Outpatient Therapy

March 17 - March 23, 2008

"It May Take 6-12 Months To Get My Stamina Back."

MY NARRATIVE

On March 18 Michelle wrote the following message on her Care Page:

"Hi everyone! I really wanted to post a short comment to let everyone know how I am doing. First, let me thank all of you for your love, support and prayers. I'm currently on my third week of outpatient rehab at Madonna and I am making progress. I don't remember the accident, hospital, or really my inpatient time at Madonna, but since I started out-patient rehab I remember the last three weeks. The long term memory is strong! I'm feeling well, but tire very easily. They told me in rehab it would take 6 to 12 months to get my stamina back. Too long, I thought. I have been working out some, which will help with the stamina. I have a big family meeting at Madonna tomorrow where I will learn how I'm doing, so wish me luck. Thanks again for thinking of me. I couldn't have made it this far without everyone's support, love and prayers."

I love you all, Michelle

PERTINENT MEDICAL NOTES
MADONNA REHABILITATION DAY PROGRAM

FAMILY MEETING: PATIENT: MICHELLE S. DATE: 3/19/08

TEAM MEMBERS ATTENDING: Social worker, Speech therapist, Occupational therapists

FAMILY MEMBERS ATTENDING: Greg – husband, Melissa – sister, Larry – father, Ruth – mother

STRENGTHS:

The occupational therapist stated that Michelle is doing well with divided attention. She felt that Michelle's visual acuity was ready for driving. According to the therapist, multitasking has improved and Michelle is ready to take over tasks such as the checkbook. Michelle will need to have someone check her work the first couple of times she does do the checkbook on her own.

The other occupational therapist stated that Michelle has done very well with house tasks. Michelle was able to do more than one task at a time. Michelle was able to maintain safety in the kitchen while doing other household tasks. The therapist stated that Michelle is doing time management skills well. The therapist stated Michelle is doing better with executive function techniques, but is still working on using the planner. There have been improvements with memory and attention, but when Michelle becomes tired or overwhelmed, attention will decrease.

NEEDS:

The occupational therapist stated that a lot of stimulation is still overwhelming for Michelle. Michelle can do a time line--has asked questions. The other therapist stated Michelle needed to continue to use energy conservation techniques and take initiative in doing these. Michelle should continue to work on short-term memory and using the planner or some other type of device. The therapist stated that by organizing days and knowing when to take a break would help manage fatigue. Michelle should continue to do pieces of the task at a time to make the task more manageable.

FAMILY QUESTIONS/CONCERNS:

Michelle feels she is improving and feels good. She states she doesn't remember the accident. She states she is able to be "mom" more at home. Michelle has been helping with baths, meals and getting the kids dressed. She states she only fixes one thing for meals rather than several trying to please everyone. Michelle states she is beginning to work out again at home. Michelle has started to take over tasks slowly like paying bills, she did one the other day. Michelle states she is able to complete the tasks lists that Greg leaves her. Michelle said she went to Target with her mom and remembered all items without a list, the kids were not with them at the time. Michelle is doing tasks with children in the evening by picking one thing that all enjoy like a puzzle or game.

Greg states that at night he tries to care for the kids so that Michelle is not overwhelmed. He states that when he gives Michelle a list, they are simple tasks and not overwhelming. Greg is concerned that the accident was medically related.

Larry states that Michelle is getting better with handling the aspect of being overwhelmed. He is still concerned about Michelle becoming mentally and physically fatigued. Larry would like Michelle to continue working on posture.

Ruth Ann states that Michelle is challenging herself more. This week Michelle addressed her own thank you cards and posted her own notes on the Care Page. Michelle did state that she takes it slow and will only do a couple of cards at a time to keep from getting tired. Mom is worried about traveling because Michelle did do this for work. Michelle did state that she traveled 3 to 5 days per month. Michelle states she usually did not travel alone. Michelle states that she worked 3 days per week prior to the accident.

Melissa states she feels that the old Michelle is coming back. She stated her personality is there, Michelle is laughing and cried about the accident recently. Melissa stated Michelle is talking about things that happened, but is unsure how far back to go with the memories. Michelle stated she was unsure how much of the accident she wanted to know about.

FOLLOW-UP PLAN:

Michelle and Greg will work on a system at home to track items for Michelle. Voc rehab is scheduled for April 1, They will assist Michelle in returning to work. She will return part-time. Therapist will work on increasing activity. Michelle will demonstrate to therapist what type of work she does through a computer program on the 20th or 21st. Michelle will do therapies Monday, Wednesday and Friday starting the week of March 24. Family will check with primary care physician about when Michelle is released medically to drive.

Chapter 24

4th week at Madonna Outpatient Therapy

March 24-March 30, 2008

Happy Easter, Everyone!

MY NARRATIVE

This week we have been giving Michelle a ride to Madonna and she is on her own for her therapies! On Monday, she told us we don't have to be with her anymore. She is comfortable going to therapy on her own. We have been keeping the same routines at home and that seems to be working out well for all of us. Keeping the children on their schedule of daycare, preschool and school gives Michelle plenty of time to rest after her mornings of therapy. I also believe it has been very good for the children to be on the same schedule they had prior to the accident.

This week, the goal of returning to work was placed on the calendar. Michelle is anxious to try to return to work and Madonna wants to assess her readiness this week.

Predicting the employability of a person with a traumatic brain injury is a very complex process. Unemployment rates vary from 10-99% of people that have suffered a traumatic brain injury. In 1998, Gollaher and colleagues reported that individuals with higher education levels and fewer disabilities from the TBI were more likely to be employed 1-3 years post-injury. Sherer and associates in 1999 found that individuals with no history of substance abuse were 8X more likely to be employed at two years post-injury. [16]

On Friday, A vocational therapist from the state went with Michelle and me to the place Michelle worked and Michelle sat at her desk and logged into her computer and looked at some of her e-mails. Michelle was quite comfortable there and tried to tell the vocational therapist about her job but since much of it is done on the computer, I don't think the therapist understood most of what she did, nor did she have any ideas about skills Michelle had to master before returning to work. Michelle was very happy to be back at work but it tired her out and we didn't stay very long.

This week is Easter week--another big challenge for Michelle. One of my good friends, who is also a past college roommate and sorority sister, has been asking me for something special she could do for Michelle. Michelle had been worrying about shopping for the kids Easter clothes. She always bought all four of them special things to wear for Easter. I asked Elaine if she would like to go shopping with Michelle and me and help Michelle pick out Easter clothes for the kids. She was thrilled to participate.

The three of us headed to the nearest shopping center and Elaine and I helped Michelle pick out dresses for Grace, Aidan and Alysen and a new shirt for Geran. Elaine insisted on also picking out socks and shoes for the girls outfits. It was Michelle's first major shopping event and she did pretty well. It was hard for her to make up her mind about things so I was glad Elaine and I were there to help her decide.

Michelle wanted to go to Greg's parents for Easter since they had come down so often to help with the family. She also wanted to spend some time with us since I always had an Easter Egg hunt for the Grands on Easter Sunday. Knowing that was a lot to try to do in one day, Michelle and Greg and the kids went to church on Saturday evening. Then on Easter Sunday morning they drove the 2 hours to Greg's parent's home and enjoyed Easter Sunday with them and other members of Greg's family. After lunch, they returned to Lincoln and came to our house for the annual Easter Egg Hunt. Fortunately, Michelle was able to sleep on the ride back to Lincoln so that helped replenish her stamina through the rest of the day.

---

16 *"Returning to Work after TBI."* September, 2007 Rainbow Visions Magazine, Rainbow Rehabilitation Centers, 5570 Whittaker Road, Ypsilanti, MI 48197. Page 1-4

Our extended families had been with us for Easter Sunday dinner so there were lots of people at our house, many of whom had not seen Michelle since the accident. They had all been following her daily progress through her CarePage but they had not had a chance to hug her and tell her how happy they were that she was overcoming the trauma of the accident.

Again, Michelle pushed herself through a very long day but she wanted to do it and Greg made it possible by suggesting church on Saturday and then having the long Sunday drives so she could get some sleep in between busy family events.

Altering schedules is so important during the recovery stages following a TBI. "The brain only heals when its resting." This phrase goes on in my head over and over. Michelle can not keep up the hectic pace that she kept prior to the accident. She has to pace herself and find quiet times for healing. The help the extended family gives in providing quiet times can not be over-emphasized. Recognizing and accepting the reality of the injury is necessary in being able to assist and facilitate recovery for our loved ones. In Michelle's case, helping her find "quiet" times in the midst of her busy family was and is a challenge. Fortunately, her job provides her with quiet work areas and few interruptions. Her job is almost a welcome respite from the rest of her busy life.

PERTINENT MEDICAL NOTES
MADONNA REHABILITATION DAY PROGRAM

NEUROPSYCHOLOGICAL SCREENING REPORT:

NAME: MICHELLE S.; AGE 38; DOMINANCE: RIGHT

ASSESSMENT RESULTS:

> On a task of sustained attention administered today, Michelle was able to obtain scores on all the primary scales within the average to high average range for both visual and auditory sustained attention abilities. Results of the RBANS-A indicate immediate memory in the lower end of average range at the 34th percentile with mild impairment in delayed memory at the 13th percentile, although fatigue seemed a large component of her impaired performance on delayed memory subtests rather than encoding. As indicated by her above average score on a list recognition subtest in which Michelle was provided a cues recall format. She obtained a language index score in the average range of 53 percentile. Michelle demonstrated moderate impairment in her visuospatial constructional ability and mild impairment in the fine motor integration on a task in which she needed to quickly scan a series of numbers and associated symbols and replace these symbols in a timed format. In terms of emotional functioning, Michelle reports no signs of depression: however, she described feelings of being overwhelmed at moments particularly when confronting the impact of the accident on her family. Michelle reports insight into the need for self-monitoring of her energy level and pacing, and she feels support from her family

Chapter 25

April, 2008

Happy Birthday, Geran! Happy Birthday, Grace!

MY NARRATIVE

This month has been quite full for Michelle and her family. Geran's 5th birthday was April 5th and Grace's 7th birthday was April 24th. Madonna had set a number of goals for Michelle before she would be released from out-patient therapy. I had set two goals for her myself.

My first goal was that she would be able to tolerate being at Geran's Birthday Party. Geran has 2 cousins whose birthdays fall within days of each other. Some years they celebrate their birthdays together and this year Greg's brother, Ken and Ken's wife Jennifer, had told us while Michelle was in the hospital that they were planning a fun birthday for Kody and Greg and Michelle should just plan on including Geran's birthday in the celebration. They also included the other cousin so a family birthday party with 3 little boys celebrating was going to be a lively event. I hoped and prayed that Michelle would be able to stand all the noise and excitement. We didn't know too much about the plans but we were told there was a rumor that some surprise guests were going to appear!

The first Sunday in April, the 3 cousins celebrated their birthdays. It was a wonderful family event with lots of food and lots of kids and lots of activity but Michelle handled it well. She was able to sit through all the excitement of opening presents, which for 3 little boys took quite a long time. After the presents were opened and everyone had ice cream and cake, the kids were moved outside to play and before long 2 figures came running down the street. Batman and Robin arrived at a neighborhood in Nebraska! They stayed about 10 or 15 minutes chatting with the kids and then took off running down the street and around the corner. They shouted back to the kids that they were returning to the "Bat Mobile" which was parked just around the corner!

It was great birthday party and Michelle made it! She was tired when it was over but she made it through all the questions about how she was feeling and how her treatments at Madonna had gone. Interestingly, she still does not remember her time as an inpatient at Madonna but does remember the last weeks when she was there for Outpatient therapy.

April 4th, Michelle was able to discontinue all therapies except Speech Therapy. She continued that once a week but was finished by the middle of April. She also passed her driving test so she was cleared to drive. None of us wanted to see her behind the wheel anytime soon but she considered it a major milestone to be able to drive--and it was!

My second goal for Michelle was that she would be able to plan Grace's birthday party. This is the type of "executive function" that Madonna uses to see if their patients are ready for the real world. It takes many pathways in the brain to call and make appointments, plan transportation, send out invitations, and coordinate birthday treats. I must say Michelle was up to it!

She let Grace invite 6 other little girls and they went to a hair salon and had their hair styled and then had manicures. I let Michelle plan the whole thing and she took care of all the details including helping Grace with the invitations and arranging rides for the girls.

I drove Michelle's car and picked up some of the girls and another mother brought the rest. The girls had a great time at the salon and Michelle was very active making sure each of the girls got the hair style they wanted and the manicures they were so excited to receive. After the salon, we took the girls to Culver's for ice cream. The party was a big success and Grace loved her Salon birthday party. Michelle had accomplished both the goals I had silently set for her during her inpatient days when her brain was really not functioning well.

Michelle had a final MRI this week and visited her neurosurgeon. Greg went with her. Michelle reports that the Doctor asked her if she remembered him. Michelle replied, "No, I don't."

He replied, "Good, I'm glad you don't remember me. I'm the guy who drilled a hole in your head and you don't need to remember any of that."

April 18, 2008 Michelle posted this on her CarePage:

"I'm happy to report that this might be my final post. I had an MRI/MRA last Friday and the results were good. My neurologist said my brain looks fine and normal. They still don't know why I hit the tree and they may never know, which is frustrating. I have graduated from Madonna Adult Rehab day program and I'm down to just Speech Pathology one day a week, with next week probably being my last time. I have returned to work, working my usual 3 days per week. Yesterday, I worked from 8:00-4:00, which is the longest I have stayed at work since the accident. Life is slowly returning to normal!

I can't tell you enough how much I have appreciated your prayers, thoughts and support. Most people with a brain injury do not recover as quickly as I have, which is probably due to all the prayers and thoughts people have been sending my way. My energy level is supposed to return in 6-12 months, I'm hoping for 3 months, but I'm not going to push it.

Thank you all so much for all the love and caring people have shown for my family and me. I would not be where I am today without it! I love you all!"

Love, Michelle

PERTINENT MEDICAL NOTES
MADONNA REHABILITATION DAY PROGRAM

PROGRESS SUMMARY: GOALS:
   1) 90% To verbalize past and future information using external communication device.
   2) 80% auditory processing for 1-2 paragraphs of information with use of strategies.
   3) 90% reading comprehension/recall for 1 page of information.
   4) 80% to complete a variety of problem solving situations with use of strategies.

LONG TERM GOALS:
   Functional use of compensatory strategies for deficits
   in cognitive/linguistic skills for return to family and work roles.
   1. 90% for verbalizing, decreased executive function. Patient reports being successful in simple home and work tasks.
   2. 80% without use of strategies, 90% with use of strategies
   3. Informal reading assessment completed. 11th 85%, 12th 90% decreased details.
   4. Numerical reasoning 75% at higher level. Planning tasks: decreased detail.
   5. Patient met 4 of 4 short term goals. Continues to demonstrate minimal recall for auditory and written information.
   6. Especially for detail, increased use of strategies and executive function. Decreased for high level work tasks.

Chapter 26

The Remaining Months of 2008

Bible School, Mayo Clinic, Family Reunion, Nebraska Football

MY NARRATIVE

    Michelle has returned to her pre-accident routine in May. She is able to drive and take the kids to school, pre-school and day care. She can work her normal 3 days per week but the company continues to monitor all her e-mails. She is able to write the "help" screens for the computer software developed by her company. She is no longer traveling for any demos but is able to do some of the demos online. When she received her first post-accident pay check, she told me the company had not taken off any of her vacation days that she had accumulated, nor had they taken any of her sick days. There are not many companies that would maintain an employee's earned time after a 3 month absence.

    June came and school was out. In some ways, that made Michelle's schedule easier. All 4 children went to the sitters on Tuesday and Thursday and came to our home on Wednesday. This schedule, however, did leave her with the children Friday, Saturday, Sunday and Monday. Four days in a row with all four kids was hard on her. Greg was there on the weekends but she still does all the food preparation, all the laundry, and most of the coordinating activities for the kids.

In June, Michelle decided she wanted the kids to have a little vacation and she selected Kansas City and Worlds of Fun. We had often gone there during the summer and our girls had loved their rides and water park. She reserved a cabin for the family at Worlds of Fun and asked us to go with them to help with the twins. I cautioned her that Worlds of Fun might be too much for her this soon after the accident but she really wanted to take them so we agreed to be part of the family vacation.

One week in June, I kept the kids Monday through Friday. I volunteered to help with Bible School at our church. I was a Crew Leader and had the twins in my crew along with a set of quads! That was fun! Bible School was each morning and I kept the kids at our house the rest of the day. The twins still took afternoon naps and after they were down, Grace and Geran and I went swimming in our backyard pool.

That same week, Michelle and Larry went to the Mayo Clinic for one more evaluation regarding her episodes of passing out. Her primary care physician thought it would be good for her to go through their neurological clinic and, frankly, we were all searching for answers as to why this happens to Michelle.

After a week at The Mayo Clinic, we have no more answers than before. The neurology department found no neurologic disorders so they referred her to the cardiology department and they gave her multiple tests and found no abnormalities. They did suggest implanting a monitor in her chest that would make a continuous record of her heart rate and they wanted her to record anytime she felt light headed or nauseous. They would then be able to study the recordings and see if they detected any abnormal rhythms.

Michelle and Larry returned to Lincoln with the good news that neurology was quite certain that she was not having epileptic seizures but with no real answers as to her medical episodes. Soon after her return from Mayo's, she had the monitor implanted in her chest by a cardiologist at the Nebraska Heart Hospital.

After the trip to Mayo's and the implant, Michelle and Greg made the correct decision to cancel their reservation at World's of Fun. They knew with all that had happened this year, Michelle didn't need to be standing in line and jockeying for position with hundreds of other people, just to get the kids on and off some rides. I was relieved they had decided to skip this vacation.

Greg loves the 4th of July. Since they live on an acreage outside of Lincoln, they can have bigger fireworks and Greg's fireworks shows do not disappoint! His brothers often join Greg's family and between the families, we have quite the display. I always make homemade ice cream and Greg usually grills steaks and burgers so it is a fun evening. Soon after the fireworks started, I looked around for Michelle. I found her sitting in the house, watching out the window, but holding her hands over her ears. The noise was too much on her "still-healing" brain.

The last Sunday in July, my side of the family had our bi-annual Troutman family reunion. The reunion was in Omaha this year and Michelle and Greg decided to attend. My dad's family was a large one, he had 2 brothers and 2 sisters and there were 19 of us cousins. We now have families that are also married and have families so we can have quite large reunions. We get together and eat and talk and catch up on the past year's events, marriages, weddings, graduations, and funerals. After that we just mingle with one another and share memories of our childhood.

I have read several books about Traumatic Brain Injuries and one of the books said brain injuries are common. If you have a large family or large extended family, you can be sure someone in your family has suffered a TBI. The book went on to say that if you are at a family reunion, look around you and you'll know the person or people that have had TBI's. They will be sitting off by themselves, preferably in a corner, while everyone else is in their little groups visiting. During the afternoon, I thought about that book and looked around for Michelle. Sure enough, there she was sitting off by herself in a chair very near a corner. Her kids would run over and talk to her once and awhile, but she was very content to just be off by herself--away from the challenge of trying to listen to the many conversations going on at once.

One day in August, Michelle was over at the house and the kids had gone swimming. Larry was with them in the pool and Michelle stretched out on the couch to rest. When Aidan and Alysen came in from swimming they immediately became hysterical and crying and running to Michelle saying, "Mommy, don't lay down, Mommy, open your eyes. Mommy, Mommy you have to get up. Please, Mommy Please." They could not be consoled until she was sitting upright talking to them and holding them in her arms. Michelle says that still happens every time she tries to lay down and just close her eyes for a minute or too. The twins just panic. They remember "Mommy ran into a tree and she went to sleep and she couldn't wake up." It has now been 6 months since the accident and they had just turned 3 but they remember it quite vividly and they can't bear to see Michelle even lean back in a recliner. Hopefully, this will pass soon.

In August, we had the good news that Lincoln Public Schools would begin accepting the students that lived on the acreages where Michelle and Greg built their home. Even better news was that Grace and Geran would be picked up each day by a school bus that stopped right at the end of their lane. They would also be dropped off at the end of their lane so Michelle's days of racing to pick up the kids from school were over. Lincoln Public Schools was opening a new elementary school close to the new high school and middle school that were already serving students in south western Lincoln. I don't even mind paying my property taxes now that my grandchildren are being picked up and dropped off from school! This is a blessing that continues to this day and I am so thankful.

September in Nebraska brings Husker Football. We are great fans and have had tickets since the south stadium was built in the early 1960's. We have six tickets together and attending games with the girls and their husbands is a much anticipated event each year. Michelle and Greg were looking forward to the season and had arranged for Greg's parent to come down and stay with the Grands during the first game. Well, Michelle made it through the first half and half-time but once the announcer began again for the 3rd quarter, the band began playing, and the crowd cheering was just too much. She said, "Mom, I can't stand it, I have to leave. I'll just go down and walk around inside the stadium." I asked her if she wanted me to go with her and she said No.

I guess this shows what kind of fans we are--we stayed and watched the rest of the third quarter! I did leave after that and went down and visited with her until the game was over. She just couldn't take being in the midst of all the fans and people. She tried one more game in November and made it a little ways into the third quarter but she had to leave again. Since then, she has worked in concessions to earn money for some of the kid's sports or she stays home and Greg brings Geran to the games. As I write this, she is going to try again this year, 2013. We'll see how it goes.

October brought more medical trauma to Michelle. She called me Saturday night and told me she had a terrible pain on her right side but high in her abdomen under her ribs. She told me it hurt so much she just had to lay in bed curled up in a little ball. She said she couldn't remember having anything that painful. This is a girl that vaginally delivered 4 kids including the twins so she knows a thing or two about pain. I told her it sounded like gall bladder to me and encouraged her to drink some hot water, sip it slowly, as hot as she could stand, and if the pain slowly went away, she had probably passed a gall stone and she should call her doctor. This is an "old wives" trick I learned from my mother who often had gall bladder "attacks" as she called them. My sister and I were instructed to heat water for her and bring her a cup of hot steaming water and she would sit and slowly sip it and somehow that eased the stone through the bile duct.

Michelle followed my advice and did get to feeling better but called the doctor and he scheduled an ultrasound for her on Monday. I was right, it was her gall bladder and it had other stones in it so October 6th, I took her to the hospital and she had surgery to remove her gall bladder. Because of her recent accident and TBI and the cardio monitor implanted in her chest, they kept her in the hospital overnight to monitor her heart rate and respirations. They had done the robotic surgery so she recovered quickly and I brought her home to our house the next day, then took her back to her home for the evening. Another old wives tale I have heard about gall bladder is that if you lose weight quickly, it can somehow trigger the formation of gall stones. I heard this in conjunction with weight loss groups. I don't know if it's true but she certainly had lost a lot of weight quickly so maybe that was a contributing factor.

Michelle recovered quickly and was totally in charge by Halloween. She got the kids the costumes they wanted. She brought them over to our house and we took them around to our neighbors, then she went across town and they went trick or treating with some of their cousins. She even took them to Grace's teacher's house because the teacher had invited all the students to come to her house and Grace <u>loves</u> her teacher and wanted to go.

December brought Christmas and all the associated activities. Michelle handled the tree decorating, home decorating, present purchasing, and gifts wrapping. We had Christmas Eve at our house and all went to church together. Then we came home and opened gifts. Michelle and Greg went to his family Christmas morning after opening gifts at their home. They had a busy two days but she is used to busy days now and that is part of her life.

January 31st, 2005, after the twins were born, the realization came to her that she had 2 newborns, a 20 month old and a 3 year old! She said, "Mom, I'm going to be tired for the next 18 years, aren't I." Of course, the answer was "Yes." However, I don't think any of us could have anticipated how much a Traumatic Brain Injury would add to the "tired" that comes from living your life every day after a brain injury.

Michelle and Greg went out with friends for New Year's Eve and we kept the kids overnight. I am sure they drank a toast to 2009 and hoped for a totally uneventful New Year!

Chapter 27

Michelle's Chapter

MICHELLE'S NARRATIVE

February 11, 2008, this date changed the lives of our family forever. The day started out like any other Monday. My husband Greg and I got up and got ready and began getting the kids up and ready to go. Grace was almost 7, Geran almost 5 and twins Aidan and Alysen three. Both Grace and Geran had school that morning and the twins had swimming lessons that day.

We piled in the car around 8:20 and headed to Wee Wisdom to drop Geran off at pre-school. Next, we drove Grace to Human Elementary where she attends first grade. Finally, the girls and I headed to the Cooper YMCA for the swim lessons. We usually pick Geran up at school at 11:30. Since swim lessons were finished at 10:00 we had time to drive over to Nebraska Mortgage where we were meeting Greg to sign papers for the refinancing of our home.

After signing the papers and saying goodbye to Greg, we loaded the girls up in my car and I headed over to pick Geran up from school. Shortly after leaving the mortgage site, the most unimaginable and unexpected thing happened.

I drove my 2001 Yukon Denali into a tree!

I have no recollection/memory of the accident or my time spent in the hospital or at

Madonna Rehabilitation Hospital. I can remember on March 1st that my in-laws were over to help, but I do not have a strong memory of what occurred that day. Also on that afternoon Greg's brother and his wife Jen and their kids came over to see how I was doing. I remember them being there but not so much what we did. Jerry and Janie (Greg's parents) went home that afternoon and we took my new Suburban out for a drive to pick up pizza.

Sunday, March 2, my sister Melissa came over to help me. She brought a puzzle for us to work on. I still do not remember the accident, and I felt like I dreamed the whole thing and that suddenly I will just wake up and this whole ordeal will have been a dream. That afternoon Greg's brother Mark, his wife Carla and their boys Conrad and Karson came over to see me as did Greg's brother Kevin and Tiffany along with their kids Dominic and Andrea. Tiffany brought pictures along of me at the hospital and a present. I set the pictures down and did not take them out of the envelope. I wasn't ready to look.

I kept staring at the envelope, and slowly, I picked it up and pulled out the pictures and took a look. I was shocked to see pictures of me lying in a hospital bed with all these machines hooked up to me. It wasn't a dream, it was real, and I couldn't remember any of it. After looking at the pictures, I finally broke down and cried. I couldn't understand why everyone was being so nice to me and doing things for me.

My sister, Melissa, had been waiting for me to cry. Throughout this whole ordeal I had not cried. She was so happy to have me finally cry. I went and sat on the sofa in the office by the fire and cried. Melissa joined me and so did my daughter Grace. Grace sat by me and cried too. I went and found Greg and cried and hugged him because I didn't understand what happened.

It was hard to come to terms with the fact that I could not remember almost 3 weeks of my life. I remember on Sunday, February 10, 2008 there was snow on the ground and the girl across the street came over to make snow forts. I know what our routine for Monday's was, but I do not actually remember it.

On the second day of outpatient therapy (I think) I met with a psychotherapist. I do not like sharing my feelings, but I went and talked and listened. Right away the therapist said I will probably never remember the accident. She said when the brain gets injured, it spends so much energy trying to heal that it picks and chooses what it wants to remember and everything else it just throws away.

I felt so much better hearing that! I could finally relax and understand why those memories were gone. My brain decided it was not important, so tossed those bad memories aside.

Chapter 28
Six Things I Wish I Had Known
and
One Thing I'm Glad I Knew!

MY NARRATIVE

1. I wish I had had a smart phone to look up meanings of medical terms after meeting with doctors and nurses!

You don't need a medical dictionary to discover the meaning of the medical terms being used during hospitalization and rehabilitation. Just a pen and paper and Google will answer most of your questions rather quickly! But, in 2008, I didn't have a smart phone and I don't think I could have connected to the internet with my phone at that time.

These are just some of the words and phrases that we had never heard before: GCS . . . Rancho Level . . . Mild Traumatic Brain Injury . . . Intraparenchymal Bleed . . . Complicated Mild Traumatic Brain Injury . . . Agnosia . . . Perseverates . . . Aphasia . . . Punctate Bleeds . . . Dysarthria . . . Basal ganglia bleed . . . Confabulation

My husband and I both worked for over 40 years in different medical fields and yet we knew virtually none of these terms. They simply floated over our heads during conversations with doctors and therapists and we were not able to find a quick, reliable source to explain them to us. BryanLGH Hospital and Madonna Rehabilitation Hospital both gave us information to read about Traumatic Brain Injuries. They were helpful little brochures, but they didn't give me the information I needed to really help Michelle.

I now know that getting them spelled correctly is the first step to finding out the meaning of words you don't understand. Ask the Doctor or the therapist to write down the words you don't understand. Actually, ask them to PRINT the words! I learned from the medical notes that handwriting can be very difficult to read so always ask them to print! Then you can simply Google the word or phrase and within moments you will have a clear understanding of the medical term that was being used to describe symptoms or injuries. No more wishing you had a medical dictionary to help you understand. Wikipedia is truly a wonderful resource and it is only a few strokes away!

2. I wish I had understood the syndrome called Post Traumatic Amnesia.

I wish I had known that Michelle wasn't remembering anything from day to day. Many people explained to me that she probably wouldn't remember the accident and I understood that right away. Frankly, I didn't want her to relive it and I know that most people do not remember their accident.

But, I didn't know she did not remember her days at BryanLGH Medical Center or her day to day activities at Madonna. After the first few days at Madonna, she knew her way around the building; she could lead the Therapists down to the gym and back. I never thought that she couldn't remember what she had done the day before. I would have used her memory book more diligently and I would have had her write things in it, too.

Not remembering from day to day brought about her fear of what people were going to do to her or what they might already have done. If I had understood the depth of her post traumatic amnesia, I would have arranged for one of us to be with her all the time. She needed someone she could trust and someone she remembered from before the accident to reassure her that she was getting better, that her therapies were helping her, and that there was a reason for the different types of therapy and how each helped her in a different way. Since she couldn't remember things from day to day, she couldn't see the progress she was making. She didn't know how much she was improving. She began to think she was doing the same things over and over again for no reason.

I could have taken her memory book and showed her, "See, the first day you walked 80 feet with someone assisting you. Now you can walk 1200 feet with no assist. You are definitely getting a lot stronger!" I would have made signs and put them on the wall.

"Monday; 80 feet, Tuesday: 120 feet, Wednesday: 430 feet, etc. I would have made visual cues for her each and every day about each activity and how much she had improved.

Because I never suspected Michelle wasn't remembering things from day to day, I was unable to provide the visual and mental help she needed. If you are going through this with a loved one, ask them questions about what they did the day before and see if they know. Find out what they remember from the day before. Give them reassurance that they are improving and their effort and hard work is being rewarded with improvement. Post improvements on a big board. Be there to help them fill in the gaps that will give them confidence in the programs in which they are participating. I believe that Post Traumatic Amnesia was the thing that was keeping Michelle from understanding the importance of her therapies. Once her PTA was gone, she participated willingly in her Outpatient Therapies and understood how much they were helping her and why she needed them.

3. I wish I would have understood how "blood in the spinal fluid" could affect many different parts of her brain and that was the cause of the random symptoms that kept her injury from really being classified specifically.

I didn't understand how her specific injury was affecting her brain. The brochures that were given us told about the different parts of the brain and how an injury in the different sections causes certain symptoms. Michelle had frontal lobe injuries from the sudden stop when her car hit the tree. The inside of the front part of the skull has rough ridges and when the brain, which is floating in spinal fluid, suddenly is projected forward because the head has stopped moving, the ridges in the skull cause damage to the frontal lobe.

In addition, she had blood in the spinal fluid which caused additional damage in some of the other areas of the brain. I never really understood her specific brain injuries until we met with her neurosurgeon after her release from Madonna. I was reading brochures that told me what happened with injury to each different area of the brain, but since Michelle had multiple contusions throughout the brain, plus the frontal lobe damage, I did not understand why she was having such random symptoms. I wish I had taken more time to questions the physicians in the hospital and I wish I had had a brochure that explained the cross-symptoms when different areas of the brain are affected.

4. I wish I had heard the term Agnosia and then I wish I had studied it for a good explanation about the symptoms it caused.

I had never heard of the word Agnosia and didn't know there was a term to describe her "phantom" symptoms--the times she would go through the motions of doing something without ever really doing them. I didn't know the word until I got the medical records for this book.

Agnosia is a word that means "lack of awareness or the inability to recognize familiar objects." I wish I had been prepared for this symptom because I have to admit, it really freaked me out! I had never seen such a thing and had no idea how long it would last or what could be done to help her overcome it. I didn't know if this was common with TBI's, if this would manifest itself in different ways, or if this was indicative of a more serious brain injury. She didn't even know it was happening until someone pointed it out to her, then she would just look devastated.

In reading her medical records from Madonna, it happened quite frequently in places like their "practice" grocery store, almost always when baking, and with me one day waiting for dinner. I think it also explains her lack of safety awareness when we left Madonna to go grocery shopping. She just walked to my car and through the parking lot not looking to the sides to look for other vehicles or cars. Even in the grocery store, she would walk quickly down an aisle pushing the grocery cart and at the last minute, swoop around to the left to a avoid a slow-moving shopper in front of her. I couldn't get her to slow down and wait for other shoppers. I wish I had been told by one of the therapists that this is common--I still don't know if it is--and what part of the brain is injured that is causing this phenomenon.

I do know that once her PTA was gone, she never exhibited any of these "phantom" activities again.

5. I wish I had known to say "yes!

I wish I had known to say "yes" more often when someone offered to help. If you have a family member in Intensive Care and you're going to be following up with Rehabilitation, you are going to need a lot of help. People really do want to help and accepting graciously lets them participate in the healing of your loved one.

Say "yes" to bringing in meals. Get plastic or paper plates and drinking cups that can be thrown away. Have serving plates ready so when someone brings in food, you can transfer it to your dishes and let them take their dishes home. That saves lots of time cleaning and trying to return dishes and trying to remember who brought what in which kind of pan. Many people do bring things in disposable containers and dispose of them! Don't waste time washing and try to save them. Keep everything moving out of your house!

Someone offered to do laundry and Greg was reluctant to have a stranger doing their laundry. I wish I would have separated the kid's clothes and let someone do those once a week for us. The kids are the ones generating mountains of clothes each day and I don't think Greg would have minded if the kids laundry was gone from the house for a couple of days each week. We spent a lot of time washing and folding and putting clothes away during the months before Michelle was able to start managing that part of household activities.

If kids are involved, take advantage of car pooling. For us, having someone pick up Grace in the middle of the afternoon each Monday just took so much stress from us. Again, people are willing to help and want to do something that really does free the care givers, so find things for friends and neighbors to do when they offer to help.

6. I will always remember "The brain only heals when it is quiet."

I left this till last, but it probably should have been first!. I wish I had known more about the healing brain and how important "down time" is for the injured person. Michelle had 4 little kids and they were very active little kids. I shudder now when I think that sometimes they would get so rowdy and loud she would go into her closet and shut the door and sit there in the dark until her head stopped hurting. I wish I had taken more days where I picked up the kids and brought them to my house all day and took them back home just before bedtime. I wish we had given her more "totally quiet" times in the early days after she came home from Madonna--particularly that first summer. I know it would have sped up the healing process and I would really like a "redo" on that first summer.

So, the last thing on my list of things I wish I had known is: **The brain can only heal when it is quiet.** It can't heal in a room full of people, it can't heal with a television blaring, and it can't heal when kids are all talking at once. It can't heal when you're talking on the phone, or when you're using an iPad or while you play a video game. It can't heal while your fixing a meal, or when your paying bills, or when you are cleaning your house or doing laundry.

The brain is busy receiving stimuli every minute of the day. The brain takes in sights, sounds, smells, touches, everything we comprehend is being handled by our brain and all at the same time while we are walking around, breathing, talking, laughing, listening. The only rest it gets is when we are sleeping or when we are alone in a quiet room with the lights turned down low and nothing is providing any stimulation at all. That is when the brain is healing. My regret is that I did not provide enough of these healing moments for Michelle.

1. One thing I'm glad I knew was the absolute importance of a good Rehabilitation Hospital.

Since Larry was a physical therapist, he knew Michelle needed the best rehabilitation we could give her and fortunately for us, there was such a place right here in Lincoln. Madonna is a nationally recognized Rehabilitation Hospital and has a team of professionals in each area of rehab--occupational, speech, and physical therapy. Their staff has a broad range of experience with patients of all ages and they design each patient's program to address the areas of that patient's weakness. Michelle's medical notes offer great insight into the kinds of therapies that were needed to help her brain heal. Recovery from a TBI depends in large part on the team of professionals coordinating the individualized care for each patient.

APPENDIX

Glossary

Agonal Respirations: Abnormal pattern of breathing characterized by gasping, and/or labored breathing. It is an extremely serious medical sign requiring immediate medical attention.

Agnosia: From Greek meaning "absence of knowledge." The loss of ability to recognize or comprehend the meaning of objects even with intact senses. Caused by damage to the occipitotemporal border.

Aphasia: From Greek meaning "speechlessness," It is a disturbance of the comprehension and formulation of language caused by dysfunction in specific brain regions.

Ataxic: Loss of coordinate voluntary muscle movements: unsteady movements and staggering gait.

Basal ganglia bleed: This is bleeding from blood vessels in an area of the brain responsible for body movements, sensation, speech, and personality. The basal ganglia is the part of the brain most frequently affected by hemorrhages, which cause blood to accumulate inside the brain, compressing and damaging the tissue.

Basilar cisterns: In neural anatomy, a cistern is any opening in the subarachnoid space of the brain created by a separation of the arachnoids and pia mater. These spaces are filled with cerebral spinal fluid.

Cerebritis: This is an infection of the brain that normally leads to the formation of an abscess within the brain itself. It's the inflammation of the cerebrum, a structure within the brain that performs a number of important functions, including most of the things which people associate with being human, such as memory and speech.

Confabulation: This is associated with poor memory. The person with a brain injury attempts to fill in the missing gaps in his earlier memory. He or she may confabulate about a situation which actually occurred by exaggerating and distorting the facts. The person confabulating due to a brain injury is unaware that what they are saying is not true.

Dysarthria: This is a motor speech disorder. The muscles of the mouth, face and respiratory system may become weak, move slowly, or not at all after a stroke or other brain injury. The type and severity of dysarthria depend on which area of the nervous system is affected

Extra-axial hemorrhage: The brain and the spinal cord are designated the neural axis. Intra-axial hemorrhage is an umbrella term for hemorrhage within the brain and spinal cord. Extra-axial hemorrhage is an umbrella term for bleeding within the cranium but outside the brain or cord parenchyma. Therefore, extra-axial hemorrhages include any or all of the epidural, subdural, subarachnoid, and intraventricular hemorrhages. Closed head trauma may cause extra-axial hemorrhage of any type or direct hemorrhage into the brain substance. As a rule these are primary lesions, beginning at the time of the injury. Although subarachnoid hemorrhage is a common finding with head trauma, epidural subdural and intracerebral hematomas are the usual expanding lesions that cause neurologic deterioration.

Fossa: A depression in the floor of the cranial vault.

Frontal parietal intraparenchymal hemorrhage: Hemorrhage in the frontal and parietal areas of the brain.

Ganglia; In neurological contexts, ganglia are composed mainly of stomata and dendritic structures which are bundled or connected. Ganglia often interconnect with other ganglia to form a complex system of ganglia known as a plexus. Ganglia provide relay points and intermediary connections between different neurological structures in the body such as the peripheral and the central nervous system.

Impaired Tissue Perfusion--Cerebral: This is related to decreased cerebral blood flow associated with space 1. Cerebral hemorrhage resulting from the underlying disease process or loss of integrity of the litigated vessels: 2. Compression of the cerebral vessels, 3. Spasm of the cerebral vessels resulting from trauma, 4. Hypotension. Symptoms may include dizziness, visual disturbances, speech impairments, decreased mental status, decreased sensory and motor functions.

Intra-parenchymal: Situated or occurring in the parenchyma of the brain.

Intraventricular hemorrhage: Occurs when there is bleeding into the spaces of the brain known as the ventricles. These spaces contain the cerebral spinal fluid.

Parenchyma: The brain parenchyma is the functional tissue of the brain. It is comprised of two type of cells that are used specifically for cognition and controlling the rest of the body. The remaining brain tissue is known as stroma, which is the supportive or structural tissue. Damage or trauma to the brain parenchyma often results in a loss of cognitive ability or even death.

Parietal/frontal: The Frontal lobe is situated at the top of the brain behind the forehead. The Parietal Lobe is behind the frontal lobe at the upper back of the skull. The Frontal Lobe controls awareness of surroundings, judgment and control of emotions, control of language and words, memory for routine tasks and habits and controls the sense of smell. The Parietal Lobe controls the ability to focus on more than one object, the ability to identify things by touch, the ability to name and use objects, and the ability to use different senses for a single purpose, for example, getting dressed.

Peduncle: The three common areas that give rise to the cerebral peduncle's are the cortex spinal cord and the cerebellum. The cerebral peduncle contains many nerve tracts conveying motor information to and from the brain to the rest of the body

Perseveration: The survivor of a brain injury may be stuck on a single topic, word, or phrase. For example Michelle was perseverating on wanting to go home. She turned every conversation into going home. She arranged her personal articles on the bed several time a day for preparing to go home. After conversations with health care personnel, she said, "See, they said I could go home" even though that had not been part of the conversation.

Punctate bleeds: Hemorrhage or bleeding occurring in minute spots.

SCD's: Sequential Compression Devices these devices help prevent deep vein thrombosis (blood clots). This therapy promotes blood flow and prevents pooling of blood in the legs.

Saccades or Saccadic eye movements: A rapid jerk like movement of the eyeball which subverts vision by redirecting the visual axes to a new location. They are quick, simultaneous movements of both eyes in the same direction.

Spatial: Refers to spatial memory which is the part of memory responsible for recording information about one's environment and its video orientation for example, spatial memory is required in order to navigate around the familiar city. Spatial memory has representations within working short-term and long-term memory. Research indicates that there are specific areas of the brain associated with Spatial memory.

Supratentorial space: The part of the brain that contains the cerebellum.

Glasgow Coma Scale [17]

The Glasgow Coma Scale is based on a 15 point scale for estimating and categorizing the outcomes of brain injury on the basis of overall social capability or dependence on others.

The test measures the motor response, verbal response and eye opening response with these values:

I. Motor Response

6 – Obeys commands for movement
5 – Purposeful movement to painful stimulus
4 – Withdraws in response to pain
3 – Flexion in response to pain
2 – Extension response in response to pain
1 – No response

II. Verbal Response

5 – Alert and Oriented
4 – Confused conversation, but able to answer questions
3 – Inappropriate words and jumbled phrases consisting of words
2 – Incomprehensible speech
1 – No sounds

III. Eye Opening

4 – Spontaneous eye opening
3 – Eyes open to speech
2 – Eyes open to pain only
1 – No eye opening

The final score is determined by adding the values of I+II+III.

Categorization:
Coma: No eye opening, no ability to follow commands, no word verbalizations (3-8)

Heat Injury Classification:
Severe Head Injury: GCS score of 8 or less
Moderate Head Injury: GCS score of 9 to 12
Mild Head Injury: GCS score of 13-15

(Adapted from: Advanced Trauma Life Support: Course for Physicians, American College of Surgeons, 1993).

---

[17] *Glasgow Coma Scale* May 9 2003. CDC: Department of Health and Human Services, Centers for Disease Control and Prevention. Retrieved on January 22, 2014 from www.bt.cdc.gov/masscasualties.

Ranchos Los Amigos Scale

There are a few different systems that medical practitioners use to diagnose the symptoms of Traumatic Brain Injury. This section discusses the Ranchos Los Amigos Scale. The Ranchos Los Amigos Scale measures the levels of awareness, cognition, behavior and interaction with the environment.

Ranchos Los Amigos Scale

Level I: No Response

A person at this level will:

Not respond to sounds, sights, touch or movement.

Suggestions for Family and Friends:

Talk quietly to your loved one.

Educate staff about familiar subjects liked by the patient, explain their personality.

Get plenty of rest and take frequent breaks.

Tell the person what you are about to do: "I'm going to brush your hair." I'm going to move your arm, it looks uncomfortable."

Level II: Generalized Response

A person at this level will:

Begin to respond to sounds, sights, touch or movement.

Respond slowly, inconsistently, or after a delay.

Responds in the same way to what he hears, sees or feels, Response may include chewing, sweating, breathing faster, moaning, moving and/or increasing blood pressure.

Suggestions for Family and Friends:

Continue the approach began at Level I.

Tell the person where they are, what happened, the date, time, and who is with them.

Tell the person that he or she is safe.

Bring favorite music to play for short periods.

Don't over stimulate with too many visitors or too much visiting.

Level III: Localized Response

A person at this level will:

Be awake on and off during the day.

Make more movements than before.

React more specifically to what he sees, hears, or feels. For example, he may turn towards a sound, withdraw from pain, and attempt to watch a person move around the room.

React slowly and inconsistently.

Begin to recognize family members and friends.

Follow some simple directions such as "Look at me" or "squeeze my hand."

Begin to respond inconsistently to simple questions with "yes" or "no" head nods.

Suggestions for Family and Friends:
- Talk to the person, not about him.
- Eliminate background noise, only one person should talk at a time.
- Talk about positive things, home events, and give him family updates.
- Answer questions over and over. Remain patient and answer questions even though they been asked many times before. The brain is confused and repetition must be expected.
- Bring in familiar objects in photographs of family members. Attach names to the back of the pictures so staff can help the person identify family members.

Level IV: Confused-agitated

A person at this level may:
- Be confused and frightened.
- Not understand what he feels or what is happening around him.
- Overreact to what he sees, hears, or feels by hitting, screaming, using abusive language, or thrashing about. This is because of confusion.
- Be restrained so he doesn't hurt himself.
- Be highly focused on his basic needs; i.e., eating, relieving pain, going back to bed, going to the bathroom, or going home.
- May not understand that people are trying to help him.
- Not pay attention or be able to concentrate for a few seconds.
- Have difficulty following directions.
- Recognize family/friends some of the time.
- With help, be able to do simple routine activities such as feeding himself, dressing or talking.

Suggestions for Family and Friends:
- Use short simple sentences and instructions.
- Correction of errors should be gentle, leading manner, such as, "I know you think your home, but this is really a hospital."
- Keep visit short and try to remain calm and reassuring. Remember the persons agitation is not personally directed but the result of his own inner confusion.
- Do not force him to do things, instead, listen to what he wants to do and follow his lead within safety limits.
- Experiment to find familiar activities that are calming to him such as listing to music, eating, etc.

Level V: Confused-inappropriate

At this level, I person may:
- Be able to pay attention for only a few minutes.
- Be confused and have difficulty making sense of things outside himself.
- Not know the date, where he is or why he is in the hospital.
- Not be able to start to complete every day activities, such as brushing his teeth, even when physically able. He may need step-by-step instructions.

Become overloaded and restless when tired or when there are too many people around; have very poor memory, he will remember past events from before the accident better than his daily routine or information he has been told since the injury.

Try to fill in gaps in memory by making things up, (confabulation)

May get stuck on an idea or activity (preservation) and need help switching to the next part of the activity.

Focus on basic needs such as eating, relieving pain, going back to bad, going to the bathroom, going home.

Suggestions for Family and Friends:

Gently correct mistakes made by the person.

Use memory aids to help the person remember information.

Repeat things as needed, don't assume that he will remember what you tell him.

Follow a schedule and keep to a routine. This is very helpful to the healing brain.

Help them organize and get started on an activity. Simple card games or puzzles may help him with his memory.

Encourage the patient to do what he can for himself, for example brushing his teeth or selecting what he wants to eat.

Level VI: Confused-appropriate

A person at this level may:

Be somewhat confused because of memory and thinking problems, he will remember the main points from a conversation, but forget and confuse the details. For example, he may remember he had visitors in the morning, but forget what they talked about.

Follow a schedule with some assistance, but becomes confused by changes in the routine.

Know the month and year, unless there is a severe memory problem.

Pay attention for about 30 minutes, but has trouble concentrating when it is noisy or when the activity involves many steps. For example, at an intersection, he may be unable to step off the curb, watch for cars, watch the traffic light, walk, and talk at the same time.

Brush his teeth, get dressed, feed himself, etc., with help.

Know when he needs to use the bathroom.

Know that he is hospitalized because of an injury, but will not understand all of the problems he is having.

Be more aware of physical problems than thinking problems

Associate his problems with being in the hospital and think that he will be fine as soon as he goes home.

Suggestions for Family and Friends:

You will still need to repeat things. Discuss things that have happened during the day to help individual improve his memory.

Encourage him regarding his therapies as he may insist that he feels fine and at this time doesn't understand the importance of the therapies to healing his brain.

Ask the team how the patient can be helped to become more independent without unnecessary frustration.

Answer questions about the accident as simply and straightforwardly as possible.

Try to keep the daily activities as simple as possible.

Talk with him about his feelings.

Level VII: Automatic-Appropriate

A person at this level may:

Follow a set schedule.

Be able to do routine self care without help, if physically able. For example, he can dress or feed himself independently; have problems in new situations and may become frustrated or act without thinking first.

Have problems planning, starting, and following through with activities.

Have trouble paying attention in distracting or stressful situations. For example, family gatherings, work, school, church, or sports events.

Not realize how his thinking and memory problems may affect future plans and goals. Therefore he may expect to return to his previous lifestyle or work.

Continue to need supervision because of decreased safety awareness and judgment. He still does not fully understand the impact of his physical or thinking problems.

Think slower in stressful situations

Be inflexible or rigid, and he may seem stubborn. However, his behaviors are related to his brain injury.

Be able to talk about doing something, but will have problems actually doing it.

Suggestions for Family and Friends:

Increase the patient's independence to care for himself by getting to therapy appointments, using memory logs, etc.

Talk to the individual as an adult.

Have the patient practice using the telephone directory and reading a map.

Take the person to a grocery store to locate a few items and then estimate what each item costs.

Be aware that judgment is still somewhat impaired.

Reinforce no driving or drinking.

Seek additional counseling and services as needed, living with a brain injury is a lifelong process.

Level VIII: Purposeful-Appropriate Stand-By Assistance

A person at this level may:

Realize that he had a problem in his thinking and memory.

Begin to compensate for his problems.

Be more flexible and less rigid in this thinking. For example, he may be able to come up with several solutions to a problem.

Be ready for driving or job training evaluation.

Be able to learn new things at a slower rate.

Still become overloaded with difficult, stressful or emergency situations.

Show poor judgment in new situations and may require assistance.

Need some guidance to make decisions.

Have thinking problems that may not be noticeable to people who did not know the person before the injury.

Suggestions for Family and Friends:

Find a support group and or counselor.

Give freedom to make choices, however, be prepared to give assistance.

Provide emotional support and encouragement.

Encourage the use of memory devices.

Organize the day to provide success such as scheduling the same time for meals, TV programs, homework and recreational activities.

Post a calendar for the rest of the family to note important dates. Discuss them frequently with the patient.

Continue to encourage asking for help when needed.

Talk to him about his feelings.

A revision of the Rancho Levels of Cognitive Functioning was developed in 1998 by Dr. Chris Hagen, one of its original authors. At the current time, Rancho Los Amigos continues to utilize the original eight level version. In the literature I received when Michelle was in the hospital one of the hospital booklets included all 10 levels, the other one only included the first eight. I have chosen to add these two additional levels and their additional information about patients long-term recovery.

Level IX: Purposeful – Appropriate Stand By Assistance on Request

A person at this level may:

Show improvement in attention skills.

Demonstrate the ability to shift back and forth between activities without help.

Be able to use his memory device, requesting help when needed.

Have difficulty anticipating problems.

Will need some assistance to help solve problems.

Show more realization to others' feelings and the consequences of his actions.

Continue to show signs of depression, irritability and low frustration tolerance at this stage.

Need additional help for socially acceptable behavior.

Suggestions for Family and Friends:

Continue to provide help as needed with memory devices.

Help the person take breaks to reduce frustration and irritability.

Encourage maximum involvement at home, in the community, at school, or work.

Keep in contact with support group and or counselors.

LEVEL X Purposeful-Appropriate Modified Independent

A person at this level may:

Be able to complete previous activities without help, but may require more time and different ways of completing the activity.

Complete several tasks at the same time without help, but requires periodic rest breaks to prevent fatigue.

Use his memory device without help.

Be able to anticipate problems and make decisions about the problem without help.

Recognize the need and feelings of others and respond in a usual, customary fashion.

Have periods of depression irritability and frustration, especially when he is tired, under stress or sick.

Suggestions for Family and Friends:

Continue to keep contact with support group and or counselors.

Encourage the person to take breaks to help reduce fatigue and frustration.

Provide education about the person and the effects of TBI to their employer or school staff.

Encourage the person to continue using their memory device.

Source
RANCHO LOS AMIGOS NATIONAL REHABILITATION CENTER

Communications Disorders Department 7601 Imperial Highway Downey, CA 60242

http://rancho.org   562-401-6690

FINDING THE RIGHT REHABILITATION PROGRAM

<u>Acute hospitals</u> provide emergency stabilization. Acute hospitals provide early treatment, stabilize complications and minimize neurological and related complications after TBI. <u>Trauma centers</u> provide an expert, coordinated team approach to trauma brain injury care. In 2009, the last year for which statistics have been released by CDC, in Nebraska 15% of males seen in the emergency room for head injuries were admitted to hospitals for trauma care. In 2009, 13% of females seen in the emergency room for head injuries were admitted to hospitals for trauma care.

Once the TBI patient is medically stable a referral may be made to the acute rehab unit within the hospital setting or to a freestanding <u>acute rehabilitation hospital</u>. It is important that the TBI patient received rehabilitation care in a setting where the team physicians, nurses, therapists and staff have expertise in management of traumatic brain injury.

After completion of an acute rehab program the individual may <u>return home</u> to the community, be referred to a <u>community based brain injury program in a residential setting</u>, return home with a referral to an <u>outpatient program</u>.

<u>Vocational rehabilitation programs</u> with TBI expertise may also be a valuable resource for returning to employment. [18]

We were fortunate in being in a city that in has one of the best Rehabilitation Programs in the United States. We never had any doubts about where Michelle should go for treatment after she was released from the acute care hospital.

For those of you that are embarking upon a search for a Rehabilitation Center that will best meet the needs of your patient, I have compiled a list of suggestions that may make your decision easier. First of all, make your list age-specific. Some centers focus on seniors, others on pediatric patients, others on teens and adults. Make sure the programs you inquire about are for the programs developed for patients the same age group as your loved one.

Relax! You won't have to answer all these questions. Most Rehab Centers will take you through their programs and explain their services and most of these items will be covered. This list is just to assist you in being thorough and making sure you have found the place that best meets the specific needs for the type in brain injury your loved one has received.

---

[18] *"Treatment Centers."* 2013 TBI Treatment Centers: Retrieved on November 2013 from www.traumaticbraininjury.com/Injury-resources/treatment-center/, Pages 1&2

1) Select a center that has exceptional experience with the type of brain injury your loved one has received. Ask for average lengths of stays--specific for the same type of brain injury your family member has sustained.

2) Based on physical capabilities of the patient; ask how many treatments will be provided each day.

3) Ask what type of treatment plans they have for the specific type of brain injury your patient will be presenting.

4) Ask to see their standard short term goals and long term goals for patients with this type of brain injury.

5) Ask to see quality outcome data on TBI programs that match your patient's injury.

6) Your loved one will be coming to the facility with a Rancho Level # that should mean specific things to the rehabilitation center. For example, if that Rancho Level is IV, ask about programs that begin at that level. (Rancho Levels are detailed in the Appendix in this book.)

7) Tour the facility. Tour the treatment areas in the facility: Is there a gym, is there a heated therapy pool, is there a practice kitchen, is there a practice community setting that includes mini stores and home setting for relearning activities of daily living?

8) Is there a 'return to work" program with vocational skills training/retraining?

9) Is there a driving program for retraining driving skills if needed?

10) Ask about the staff, what are the credentials, how many Physical Therapists, how many Speech Therapists, how many Occupational Therapists? Are there social workers, case managers, nurses, physicians, recreations specialists, chaplains?

11) What is the average number of years their case managers and department heads have been working at this facility?

12) Is the facility accredited by CARF (an international rehabilitation accreditation commission) for inpatient and outpatient spinal cord, brain injury, pediatric family centered and stroke specialty programs as well as comprehensive inpatient and outpatient programs, including patients and/or neurological conditions. Note, rehab centers are not required to be CARF accredited. Many want this accreditation as it provides assurance to the public that the facility has been inspected and meets the guidelines established by the CARF accrediting body.

13) Will this rehabilitation facility accept your health insurance?

14) Will they allow your primary care physician to follow the care given your loved one and will they send your primary care physician information regarding the patient's care?

15) Will they allow family to accompany the patient to treatments?

16) Will they allow family to stay overnight with the patient?

17) Ask for an anticipated length of stay.

18) Ask how often you will be involved with team meetings that include therapists that are working daily with your loved ones.

If you are in an area of the country where there are no close Rehabilitation Centers, your physicians at the Acute Hospital probably have some suggestions about treatment centers. You can also do some research by going to the Brain Injury Association website www.biausa.org and click on "Find BIA in your state." You will be taken to your state's BIA organization and click on the "contact us" option. Your state's BIA organization will come up along with a phone #. Call the organization and explain your specific needs and they should be able to help you with a list of the Rehab Centers that are close to you.

IS THIS A CONCUSSION?

In 1945, at 3:00 in the afternoon, I was riding in the back end of my Dad's pickup when he stopped for oncoming traffic before making a left turn across traffic into our farm. While waiting for oncoming traffic to clear, a drunk driver ran into the back end of our pick-up throwing me out onto the gravel road upon which we were waiting. I landed on my face in the gravel.

I was 4 years old at the time and I remember my Dad holding me in the car. Someone else was taking us to our small town doctor's office, and I remember Daddy holding me tight and saying, "Say, Daddy, Say, Daddy" but I just couldn't say it. I remember the bright light in my eyes as the doctor cleaned gravel out of cuts on my face and also around my teeth. They say you don't remember pain and I don't, I just remember thinking, "If I scream louder, maybe they will turn off that light and leave me alone!"

I still have a few scars on my face but they blend in with the "laugh lines." I have some "self-fused" vertebrae in my neck but no one thought about neck or head injuries since I was screaming and thrashing around trying to get away. Did I have a concussion or perhaps even a TBI? To this day, I do not like classical music, "it hurts my head!" Now that I know about TBI's, I blame that accident for my inability to enjoy classical music!

In 1971, my oldest daughter came screaming in the house to tell me our 3 year-old Melissa was hurt. I ran to our back yard and she way laying on the sidewalk by our backyard gate. She was sobbing holding her head and as I pulled her hand away I saw a typical "concrete kiss" on her forehead. She had ridden her tricycle over to the gate, then proceeded to stand up on the seat and she tried to reach the lock so she could go out and ride in the driveway. Of course, as she reached, the tricycle rolled backwards away from the gate and down she went on the sidewalk.

I called our pediatrician and he recommended we take her to the emergency room and have her x-rayed to make sure she did not have a skull fracture. We did this--she did not have a skull fracture. The next morning when she woke up, her right eye looked like a black golf ball was sitting in her eye. During the night, blood had drained from somewhere into that eye socket. Had she suffered a concussion? The word TBI wasn't even in our vocabulary yet. She suffered no other ill effects and the black eye was gone in a few weeks.

Life happens and throughout life, we all strike our head on something. When is it a concussion? How can we be sure? The following information about concussions may provide some insights into this injury.

A concussion is a type of brain injury caused by a bump, blow, or jolt to the head that can change the way your brain normally works. Concussions can also occur from a fall or a blow to the body that causes the head and brain to move quickly back and forth. Healthcare professionals may describe a concussion as a "mild" brain injury because concussions are usually not life-threatening. Even so, their effects can be very serious and can lead to future disabilities. [19]

A mild blow or jolt to the head or body may cause the brain to rotate or suddenly shift within the skull. When the brain receives this sudden movement, stretching and tearing of brain cells may occur. Physical, emotional, and cognitive symptoms may be the result of these changes inside the brain. A concussion affects how the brain works. It is a problem of function, not structure. This is why brain CT scans and the standard MRI results are normal with most concussions. This is also why a concussion is difficult to diagnosis. [20]

The Human Brain weighs about 3 lbs. It has the consistency of soft gelatin or soft tofu. The largest part of the brain is called the Cerebral Cortex and it consists of 4 major lobes, the Frontal Lobe, the Parietal Lobe, the Temporal Lobe, and the Occipital Lobe. The Cerebral Cortex alone contains 200 billion neurons with 125 trillion synapses. The brain is the fattest organ of the body and is 75 % water. It floats inside the skull suspended in about 1 cup of spinal fluid. The brain is fully developed by age 18 and begins to decline by age 25.

There are left and right hemispheres in the brain The right hemisphere controls the left side of the body, movements and feelings as well as drawing, musical abilities, and intuitive interpretation of other people feelings or emotions. The left hemisphere controls movements and feelings on the right side of the body and speaking, reading and writing and understanding what is said. Each hemisphere is divided into four parts or lobes. The Frontal Lobes are involved in formation of personality and help with problem solving and implementation. The Temporal Lobes help us learn, remember, and understand information. The Parietal Lobes are the touch, read, and "understand what the eyes see" part of the brain. The Occipital lobes control vision. [21]

---

19 "Brain Injury Definitions." 2010. Brain Injury Association of Nebraska. Retrieved on November 14, 2013 from www.biane.org/what/

20 "Oregon Concussion Awareness and Management Program (OCAMP), Straight Talk about Concussion: It's a Brain Injury. It's serious." Page 1. Retrieved January 20, 2014 from www.Brain101.orcasinc.com.

21 The Human Brain, Wikipedia. The Free Encyclopedia Retrieved March25, 2014 from http://en.wikipedia.org/wiki/Human_Brain

It is easy to imagine how much damage can be done to the brain by even a small blow or jolt that sends it careening into the hard skull. Once the damage is done, the brain is subject to further injury, and added stress can bring about more symptoms until the brain in fully healed. Some studies have suggested that it usually takes brain cells 7 to 10 days to recover but some symptoms may last a month.[22]

Even though symptoms may appear mild, children and teens that suffer a concussion take longer to recover than adults. A concussion can lead to significant lifelong impairment affecting a person's memory, behavior, learning, and emotions. For young athletes with a concussion, full recovery is dependent on quick diagnosis, proper management and education of both parents and coaches. Recreation related concussions led to a 60% increase in the emergency room visits during the last decade. Overall the greatest number of brain injury related emergency room visits includes bicycling, football, basketball and soccer.[23]

From birth to nine years the most common brain injuries happen during playground activities or while bicycling. 71% of all sports or recreation related brain injuries that resulted in an emergency room visits were among males. 70.5% of these emergency room visits were among persons aged 10 to 19 years old. For males aged 10 to 19, the most common causes of these brain injuries were playing football or bicycling. For females aged 10 to 19, the most brain injuries occurred while playing soccer, basketball, or while bicycling.[24]

These are the following symptoms of a concussion:

    Headache or pressure in the head

    Nausea or vomiting

    Balance or blurry vision

    Bothered by light or noise

    Feeling sluggish, hazy foggy or groggy[25]

---

22 Rusty McKune MS, ATC. University of Nebraska Sports Medicine Program Coordinator. "Return to Learn: Bridging the Gap between Concussion and the Classroom." 7th Annual Nebraska Brain Injury Conference. Younes Conference Center, Kearney, Nebraska   April 4 & 5, 2013. Lecture

23 "Concussion in Sports and Play: Get the Facts." October 6, 2011 Centers for Disease Control and Prevention Retrieved on November 14, 2013 at www.cdc.gov/concussion/sports/facts.html

24 "Concussion in Sports and Play: Get the Facts." October 6, 2011 Centers for Disease Control and Prevention Retrieved on November 14, 2013 at www.cdc.gov/concussion/sports/facts.html

25 "Signs and Symptoms of a Concussion." Brain Injury Association of Nebraska. Retrieved on November 7, 2013 from www.biane.org/sports/concussionsymptoms.html.

Symptoms usually clear up within 7 to 10 days but they may last up to a month. Returning to play and full-time academics before symptoms are cleared can result in prolonged time of recovery and risk of further injury. For recovery, rest is critical. The first several days, complete cognitive and physical rest is needed for the brain to heal. This means no TV, no video games, no tablets or smart phones. Quiet time in a darkened room and sleep are the best ways to promote healing. Most cases subside after a few weeks if student's life activities are adjusted. The first step should be returning to the classroom. If the student complains of headaches or problems seeing or is just stressed by returning to academics he/she should remain at home till symptoms again subside. Return to play can only happen when the student is symptom-free in the classroom. [26]

New research indicates that young athletes are particularly vulnerable to the effects of concussion/mild brain injury. Youth appear to be at increased risk for repeat injuries and disability. 90% of second injuries occur within 10 days of the first because the student returns to regular activities too soon. If the brain is not completely healed, reactions times are slower, making repeat injury more likely. After one brain injury, the risk for a second is 3X greater. After the second injury the risk for a third injury is 8X greater.[27]

Many universities and states are scrambling to deal with the increased incidence of concussions. In 2012, the Nebraska State Legislature passed the Nebraska Concussion Awareness Act. Under the law, an athlete showing signs or symptoms of a concussion, thereby being "reasonably suspected" of having had a concussion, must be removed from participation and may not return until evaluated by a licensed health care professional.

The law passed by the Nebraska State Legislature has three requirements:

1) Education: All coaches, youth athletes, and their parent or guardian must be provided with education about the risks and symptoms of concussion and how to seek proper medical attention.

2) Removal from play: Under any reasonable suspicion of concussion, coaches will remove youth athletes from play.

3) Return to play: Youth athletes will not be allowed to return to play including games, scrimmages, and practices of any kind, until written approval from an appropriate licensed health care professional AND the youth's parent or guardian is obtained.

---

26 Rusty McKune MS, ATC. University of Nebraska Sports Medicine Program Coordinator. "Return to Learn: Bridging the Gap between Concussion and the Classroom." 7th Annual Nebraska Brain Injury Conference. Younes Conference Center, Kearney, Nebraska April 4 & 5, 2013. Lecture

27 Rusty McKune MS, ATC. University of Nebraska Sports Medicine Program Coordinator. "Return to Learn: Bridging the Gap between Concussion and the Classroom." 7th Annual Nebraska Brain Injury Conference. Younes Conference Center, Kearney, Nebraska April 4 & 5, 2013. Lecture

Licensed health care professional may be a physician, physician's assistant, nurse practitioner nurse, athletic trainer, neuropsychologists, or any licensed healthcare worker in Nebraska who is specifically trained in pediatric traumatic brain injury.[28]

Oregon's legislature passed a law called Max's law. It was named for Max Conradt, a high school quarterback that at the age of 17 suffered a concussion while playing football. With no medical confirmation that his first concussion had cleared, Max started the next game. At half time he collapsed and was found to have massive bleeding in his brain even though he had taken no hits during the first half of the game. Max had to endure three critical brain surgeries but his life was saved. He was in a coma for three months. Once he became physically stable Max began a long period of rehabilitation. He now lives in a group home for individuals with brain injuries in Salem, Oregon.[29]

Max's Law requires Oregon school districts to implement new concussion management guidelines for student athletes. Successful concussion management policies follow the Recognize, Remove, Refer, Return protocol.

The Oregon Center for applied science now known as ORCAS adapted the recommendations of the Oregon Concussion and Management program (OCAMP) and the Slocum Sports Concussion Program and prepared a flow sheet for following concussions of school-age children. I am including this adaptation in this chapter because I think it provides specific information on how concussions should be followed for both young athletes injured in sports activities and for youth that are injured in accidents while biking or on the playground.[30]

---

28 "Signs and Symptoms of a Concussion." 2010 Brain Injury Association of Nebraska. Retrieved on November 7, 2013 from www.biane.org/sports/concussionsymptoms.html
29 "Oregon Concussion Awareness and Management Program (OCAMP),
Straight Talk about Concussion: It's a Brain Injury. It's serious." Retrieved January 20, 2014 from www.Brain101.orcasinc.com.
30 "Oregon Concussion Awareness and Management Program (OCAMP),
Straight Talk about Concussion: It's a Brain Injury. It's serious." Retrieved January 20, 2014 from www.Brain101.orcasinc.com.

RETURN TO ACADEMICS PROGRESSION

Progression is individual. All concussions are different. Students may start at any of the steps, depending on symptoms, and may remain at a step longer if needed. If symptoms worsen, the Concussion Management Team should reassess. If symptoms quickly improve, a student may also skip a step or two. Be flexible

Steps	Progression	Description
1	Home- Cognitive and physical rest	Stay at home No driving Limited mental exertion-computer, texting, video games, homework
2	Home-Light Mental Activity	Stay at home No driving Up to 30 minutes mental exertion No prolonged concentration

Progress to step 3 when student handles up to 30 minutes of sustained mental exertion without worsening of symptoms.

Steps	Progression	Description
3	School: Part Time Maximum adjustments Shortened day/schedule Built in breaks	Provide quiet place for scheduled mental rest Lunch in a quiet environment No significant classroom or standardized testing Modify rather than postpone academics Provide extra time, help, and modified assignments

Progress to step 4 when student handles 30 to 40 minutes of sustained mental exertion without worsening of symptoms.

Steps	Progression	Description
4	Part Time Moderate adjustments Shortened day/schedule	No Standardized testing Modified classroom testing Moderate decrease of extra time, help, and modification of assignments

Progress to step 5 when student handles 60 minutes of mental exertion without worsening of symptoms.

Steps	Progression	Description
5	School -Full Time	No standardized testing: routine tests OK. Minimal adjustments Continued decrease of extra time, help, and modification of assignments May require more support in academically challenging subjects

Progress to step 6 when student handles all class periods in succession without worsening of symptoms AND receives medical clearance for full return to academics and athletics.

Steps	Progression	Description
6	School -Full Time Full academics No adjustments	Attends all classes Full homework and testing

When symptoms continue beyond 3 to 4 weeks, prolonged in-school supports are required. Request a meeting with Concussion Management Team to plan and coordinate student supports.

RETURN TO PLAY PROGRESSION

Return to play is a medical decision. The concussion management team will be familiar with state concussion laws and understand which healthcare providers may clear a student. To begin the return to play plan, the student must be free of all symptoms, have no academic adjustments in place, and be cleared by a healthcare provider. The student may spend 1-2 days at each step before advancing to the next. **If post-concussion symptoms occur at any step, stop activity and have the Concussion Management Team reassess.**

Rehabilitation Stage	Functional exercise at stage of rehabilitation	Objective of stage
1. No activity	Symptom-limited physical and cognitive rest	Recovery
2. Light aerobic exercise	Walking, swimming or stationary cycling keeping intensity <70% maximum permitted heart rate. No resistance training	Increase Heart Rate
3. Sport-specific exercise	Skating drills in ice hockey. Running drills in soccer. No head impact activities	Add movement
4. Non-contact training	Progression to more complex drills, coordination and training drills, e.g. passing drills in football and ice hockey. May start progressive resistance training.	Exercise, cognitive load
5. Full-contact Practice	Follow medical clearance and participate in normal training activities	Restore confidence. Assess functional skills by coaching staff
6. Return to play	Normal game play	

Recommendations from 2012 Zurich Consensus Statement on Concussions-McRory, P., Meeuwisse, WH, Aubry, M. et al., Sports Med 2013 47:250-258. [31]

---

[31] "Oregon Concussion Awareness and Management Program (OCAMP), Straight Talk about Concussion: It's a Brain Injury. It's serious." Retrieved January 20, 2014 from www.Brain101.orcasinc.com.

Although these guidelines seem rather onerous at first glance, protecting the brain and giving it a chance to heal completely must be the goal for every person suffering a brain injury.

The University of Nebraska recently completed a $55 million upgrade to the east side of the football stadium. In addition to adding 38 luxury suites and an additional 6,000 seats for football fans, the University included space for a project called the University of Nebraska's Center for Brain, Biology, and Behavior. CB3, as it is called, is one of the university-affiliated research centers across the nation looking for better ways to diagnose and treat concussions and traumatic head injuries.

There are about 300,000 sports-related concussions reported in the United States annually, Dennis Molfese, the director of the Nebraska program, was recruited from the University of Louisville. He was given carte blanche in the design and equipping of CB3. Molfese is among 14 experts serving on the National Academy of Sciences Institute of Medicine Committee on Sports-Related Concussions in Youth, which will report to Congress and the President on brain injuries in children and young adults. He also is the chairman of the Big Ten-Ivy League partnership studying brain injuries in sports.

Nebraska's brain center is connected by a 100-foot skywalk to the new Athletic Performance Lab, which will research, among other things, injury prevention and high tech ways to maximize performance of athletes. CB3 and the performance lab will partner on some projects.

CB3's main attraction is an MRI machine, known as a functional MRI, which can track the brain's blood flow. It is hoped the scanner helps to better define what is and is not a concussion. Molfese says the sideline concussion assessment tool would be the first of what he hopes are many groundbreaking developments to come out of CB3. The device would go far beyond the standard practice of asking injured athletes questions and judge, based on his or her answers, whether it is safe for him or her to return to the game. The director said the device could be ready in one to two years, and eventually could also be used in hospitals to screen patients for head injuries. [32]

In June 2012 the Army announced that it is now running blood tests similar to the one used to test blood sugar that can be used by medics on the battlefield to determine if a soldier has sustained damage to brain cells and has experienced a concussion or a traumatic brain injury. The protein they have found to be the most sensitive and specific

---

32 Olson, Eric. :University of Nebraska's new CB3 Research Center Will Study Concussions. July 4.2013, Retrieved on February 3, 2014,from www.huffingtonpost.com/2013/07/05/university-of-nebraska-concussions-cb3-research.

for acute brain injury is called UCHL1 or ubiquitin carb oxyl-terminal esterase L1 or GFAP or glial fibrillery acidic protein. [33]

November 19, 2013 the University of Pennsylvania's Perlman School of Medicine posted a news release that they had developed a blood test that accurately diagnoses concussion and predicts long-term cognitive disability. The protein they are testing is called calpain-cleaved all-spectrin N-terminal fragment (SNTF). This protein was present in levels that were twice as high in patients following a traumatic brain injury. The blood tests given on the day of the mild traumatic brain injury showed 100% sensitivity to predict concussions leading to persistent cognitive problems and 75% specificity to correctly rule out those without functional harmful concussions. These initial findings will be followed up with larger studies but perhaps the future is very near for diagnosing concussions and TBI's on athletic fields, on the battlefields, and following head injuries. This early diagnosis should allow healthcare professionals to correctly diagnose and recommend appropriate treatment plans for their patients suffering head injuries. [34]

Quick diagnosis of brain injuries combined with professionally guided rehabilitation is the key to maximum recovery for patients that suffer from these life-changing accidents. Research is being done in many areas to provide tests that will accurately and quickly diagnose brain injuries. Better diagnosis will lead to better treatments and better outcomes and in the long term will save lots of dollars. These changes can't come soon enough for the 1.7 million people that suffer brain injuries each year.

---

33 McIlvanie, Rob.(June 6, 2012) "Trials for Traumatic Brain Injury blood test underway." The United States Army. Retrieved May 8, 2014 from www.army.mil/article/81204/Trials_for_traumatic_brain_injury_blood_test_underway/

34 "Blood Test Accurately Diagnoses Concussion and Predicts Long Term Cognitive Disability" Perelman School of Medicine/University of Pennsylvania Health System November 19, 2013. Penn Medicine News Release. Retrieved on January 10, 2014 from www.upenn.edu/news/News_Releases/2013/11/siman/

MICHELLE'S MEDICAL EPISODES

I am including this document of Michelle's episodes because she still does not have a diagnosis other than neurocardiogenic syncope. It is our hope that perhaps others that have had similar episodes and will also have experienced this type of pattern. Maybe there is a common thread to explain why this happens.

History of medical episodes (fainting) for Michelle

August 27, 2010. Michelle had the feeling of nausea that she gets prior to fainting and she sat down in the kitchen. She reports sitting there about 5-10 minutes until the feeling passed. She then finished cleaning her kitchen and went to the bathroom. She remembers standing up from the toilet but nothing else. She fell forward and either hit the door knob or the floor and broke her nose and suffered a cut that required stitches. Her husband took her to BryanLGH West for emergency care. Ten days after the accident, she had surgery to repair her nose. She was ordered to follow up with her primary care physician.

Note: Michelle had been training to run/walk a marathon in San Francisco for the Leukemia Foundation. On Saturday, prior to the accident, she had run one of her training protocols.

March, 2010. I (mother) received a call from Michelle asking me to come to work and pick her up. She had had one of her episodes and was unable to continue working. I arrived to pick her up and one of her co-workers had been taking her blood pressure and reported that each time Michelle tried to get up, she would pass out again. They couldn't get her beyond sitting up. I went to get the car and they came outside and told me she had passed out again and we called 911 and she was transported to BryanLGH West. We took the blood pressure readings with us and it was determined that low blood pressure was the reason for the episode and she was released to follow up with her primary care physician.

Note: Michelle had been training to run/walk in the 1/2 marathon that was being held in Lincoln in May. She did walk the 1/2 marathon in May.

Notes from Michelle: When I first felt nauseous in March my reading was 104 / 48 pulse 58, I laid down and took another reading and it was 119 / 50 pulse 68. I felt nauseous again and my blood pressure was 85 / 50 pulse 58 and I laid down on the floor again and it was 106 / 47 pulse 65. Marcia elevated my feet and my reading was 120 / 66 pulse 72.

At 11:30 I passed out and Marcia took the following readings:
- 101 / 62 pulse 62
- 117 / 62 pulse 61
- 120 / 69 pulse 62
- 119 / 61 pulse 59
- 113 / 62 pulse 63
- 112 / 62 pulse 64

For all the above reading my feet were elevated. Marcia had me lower my feet and the reading was 120 / 60 pulse 60.

I got up and then I threw up and my readings were:
- 146 / 113 pulse 96
- 130 / 67 pulse 69
- 124 / 67 pulse 68
- 122 / 66 pulse 79

For the above reading I was sitting. Then the ambulance came and took me to Bryan LGH. I also threw up in the ambulance.

February 11, 2008. Michelle was driving their SUV and suddenly veered across 4 lanes of traffic and drove into a tree. After the accident she was unconscious and taken to BryanLGH trauma center. She had surgery and a probe placed in her brain to monitor pressure. She had suffered a traumatic brain injury and was in intensive care 4 days, in Madonna Rehabilitation Hospital 3 weeks and had outpatient therapy at Madonna for an additional 8 weeks. MRI's showed damage in the frontal lobe that could lead to seizures and she was on seizure meds for the rest of 2008 and all of 2009. She discontinued these meds in February, 2010, as her neurologist felt she did not need to be on them any longer.

Note: It has not been proven that the accident was caused by one of her medical episodes since Michelle cannot remember the accident or the moments leading up to the accident. She does not know whether or not she had the feeling of nausea before the accident.

May, 2007. Michelle called parents and asked for help. She was home alone with the twins and picked up one out of her high chair and passed out. Fell in kitchen, child was not hurt. Crawled into play room with twins until help arrived. She mentioned having had diarrhea several times that day. No further episodes in 2007. Became pregnant in April 2004, Gave birth to twins in January, 2005. No episodes in 2004 or 2005.

Fall 2002

Michelle spent 72 hours in the seizure clinic at Immanuel Hospital for evaluation of her "episodes." All testing was normal and the neurologist felt she did not have epilepsy.Became pregnant in August, 2002. Gave birth in April, 2003, to a son. No episodes in 2003.

Tuesday, May 28, 2002

Michelle went to work and had another episode about 9:00 am. She was sitting at her desk and stayed in her chair. Her feet went out in front of her and pointed inward, her extremities twitched. She was out perhaps 30 seconds. Her husband came and picked her up and took her to the doctor.

Monday, May 27, 2002, during the night Michelle got up and went to the bathroom. When she laid down, she remembers feeling nauseous. The next things she remembers, he husband thought she was gasping for air, her eyes were open and she was stiff. He was worried that perhaps she was not breathing.

Monday, May 27, 2002 10:30 am Michelle came to parents home to do laundry and move some things to their new home. She brought Grace to mother and asked me to watch her while she carried some things to the car. She returned to the family room (upper level). About 10 minutes later she came downstairs saying she thought she had just had another episode. She felt nauseous, sat down on the floor, and then came to with her head against the piano bench. The piano bench had been knocked over. She did not feel well and had to lie down. She stayed down for almost an hour.

Thursday: November 15, 2001 While onsite with a client in Salt Lake City, I (Michelle) felt very nauseous while sitting at a desk in front of a computer terminal. Michelle's account: "The next thing I remember someone was touching my shoulder asking me if I was OK. I don't have any recollection of falling or passing out. There were 2 women in the room with me when it occurred. One reported my arms slightly twitching, and the other reported that I did not appear to be breathing. When I came to, after about 30 seconds, I was breathing normally, was not tired, and was able to stand on my own. I had hit the bridge of my nose on the way down and they took me to the emergency room."

Saturday: October 6, 2001 2:30 Laundry Room, Michelle walked up to dryer to unload dryer, felt light headed and nauseous. Turned sideways and put hand on knees. Heard garage door open and close. I (Michelle's mother) came in garage door and walked into kitchen. Heard a loud thump in utility room. Went in and found Michelle lying on floor with head in corner between the wall and the counter. Her nose was smashed against the cupboard door, I could only see the right eye, and it was open and rolled back. Her body was tense and extremities twitched several times, toes were turned inward. She was out maybe 30 seconds. When she came to she said, "Where am I, Where am I? What happened." I told her I thought she had had another episode. She immediately said she had to go lay down, she didn't feel good. She went to her room and laid down on her bed. I hugged her and kissed her face and she said, "Don't do that, my head hurts too much to be held." She stayed in bed about 10 minutes. Grace woke up so she got up. Larry took her blood pressure, she was seated on a bed. It was 124/62.

Activities prior to episode: 12:00 emptied kitty litter—it was overdue for cleaning and had very strong odor. 12:30 Balanced checkbook 1:00 Fed Grace and played with Grace. 1:45 Put Grace to bed. Started doing laundry. Monday through Friday: Training seminar in Utah.

After episode: Michelle wanted to spend time with Grace since she had been gone so we took Grace downstairs and let her play on a quilt with some toys. Michelle laid beside her. At some point she said, "I can't keep laying here, I feel nauseous. She sat up and leaned her back against a recliner. (about 3:30 pm) Within moments she started staring straight ahead and leaning to the left. I (Mother) put my arms around her. Her father (a physical therapist) was in the room with us and he also observed "hypertonicity" and slow rhythmic spastic movements. This episode lasted maybe 15 seconds.

We called her doctor and he said to take her to the hospital for observation. We called her husband and waited for him to get to the house to take her to the hospital.

4:10. Preparing to go to the hospital, Grace was in her car seat, Michelle was on a chair facing the car seat. Michelle suddenly fell forward into the car seat with her face on Grace. Michelle's father leaned her back up into her chair. The same movements were again observed, slow rhythmic movements or twitches. This episode lasted about 15 seconds.

5:00 Hospital. Felt nauseous once in the hospital but did not have an episode. Hospital reported urinary tract infection. Michelle felt sure she did not have a bladder or UTI infection and she noted that the nurse that took her urine sample did not write her name on the urine cup. I (Mother is a medical technologist) collected a urine sample at home and took it to the lab where dipstick showed nothing abnormal and culture in 24 hours showed no growth. Preliminary dx at hospital—vago-reaction that could be caused by bladder infection. Follow up with Dr.

April 27, 2001. Michelle had given birth to a baby girl April 24, 2001. In the morning, Michelle took a shower, ate cereal, fed Grace and we put Grace into her crib in her bouncy chair to watch her mobile. Michelle got their video camera and took some pictures of her watching her mobile. We decided to put Grace's clothes away that she had gotten while in the hospital. We got a chair for Michelle to sit on. She was going to tell me where to put the clothes. I picked up a pink dress and asked her if she wanted it to be hung up or in the drawer and she didn't answer. I looked at her and she was sort of staring straight ahead. I asked her if she was ok, she said, no, I don't feel good. I said, "Do you think you're going to throw up." Michelle: "Maybe". I ran less than 6 feet away and grabbed a waste paper basket. When I came back, she was staring straight ahead and could not speak. I put my arms around her shoulders because I thought she was going to faint and I wanted to hold her in the chair. Instead, her legs just went out slowly in front of her, her feet turned inward, and her arms went stiff at her sides. She then "twitched" 3 or four time. Then she slowly brought her legs back up by the chair and brought her arms back into her lap. She asked me what happened. I told her I thought maybe she had fainted

(I didn't want to scare her.) She said she didn't feel good at all and needed to lay down. As we walked into the bedroom she said, "Mom, that's how a felt when I was talking to Sarah." I called doctor and husband and she was admitted to BryanLGH East.

June 2000: At work, suddenly felt nauseous, went to bathroom, had diarrhea, threw up. Almost passed out. Went to the emergency room. Had pregnancy test, EEG, MRI, and heart monitor and hormone assays.

March 2000: Home alone, had just taken shower and dried her hair. The phone rang and she was on the phone with best friend Sarah. She was standing at her closet deciding what to wear. Suddenly felt nauseous, told Sarah she didn't feel good and needed to lay down. Next thing she heard was Sarah yelling, "Michelle, Michelle, Michelle, talk to me." Sarah estimates she was away from the phone 30–60 seconds. Michelle felt sick afterwards and stayed in bed most of the rest of the day.

January, 2000: Michelle had the flu, she had thrown up the evening before and so she had not eaten anything for 24 hours. She felt better in the morning and got up to take a shower. She was just rinsing her hair and the next thing she knew, she was lying on the floor in the bathroom with the shower curtain around her. She had a "rug burn" on her chin. That evening, she got out of bed to go to the bathroom, she put her feet on the floor and felt nauseous. The next thing she knew, she was on the floor twisted up in her comforter (which had been on the bed). She does not remember anything between sitting on the side of the bed and finding herself on the floor.

Current Update:

Michelle has not has an episode since 2010. She had a 5 hour glucose tolerance test. The results follow:

Fasting: 93

1 hour: 104

2 hour: 105

3 hour: 88

4 hour: 54

5 hour: 79

This is not a normal Glucose Tolerance test but it also not typical for a diagnosis of hypoglycemia. A normal glucose tolerance test goes up over 120 after drinking a sugary solution. It should then have returned to normal by hour 2 and by hour three should remain normal.

Michelle's test barely went above fasting levels--which should be 100 or below. Her four hour glucose was low and in a typical hypoglycemic patient, the 5 hour would be lower, perhaps below 50.

So, Michelle's glucose tolerance was not diagnostic for hypoglycemia but it certainly was not normal. Michelle decided to eat like a hypoglycemic--5 or 6 small meals throughout the day and she only eats sweets after she has had proteins and carbs. In other words, if she eats a dessert at all, she only eats it after she has had a good meal.

Following this voluntary eating plan, she has not had any more episodes nor has she had any nauseous feelings that she used to get right before she passed out. We believe that her low blood pressure, her slow heart rate, and her unusual glucose tolerance may all work together in such a way that when they all hit their low threshold at once, she passes out.

This is only a theory but we would be interested to know if anyone else that suffers from these medical episodes has ever had a 5 hour glucose tolerance test or ever had a glucose run immediately post episode.

To share information regarding similar medical episodes, please contact us at:

rabartels19@gmail.com

BIBLIOGRAPHY

1) "Blood Test Accurately Diagnoses Concussion and Predicts Long Term Cognitive Disability" Perelman School of Medicine/University of Pennsylvania Health System November 19, 2013. Penn Medicine News Release. Retrieved on January 10, 2014 from www.upenn.edu/news/News_Releases/2013/11/siman/

2) "Brain Injury Definitions." 2010. Brain Injury Association of Nebraska. Retrieved on November 14, 2013 from www.biane.org/what/

3). Chan, Jeffrey; Parmenter, Trevor/ and Stancliffe. Volume 8, Issue 2, 2009. *"The Impact of Traumatic Brain Injury on the Mental Health Outcomes of Individuals and Their Family Care Givers."* Australian e-Journal for the Advancement of Mental Health Pages 2-7

4) "Concussion in Sports and Play: Get the Facts." October 6, 2011 Centers for Disease Control and Prevention Retrieved on November 14, 2013 at www.cdc.gov/concussion/sports/facts.html

5) Forman CM, Vasey, PA Lincoln, NB (2006) *"Effectiveness of an adjustment group for brain injury patients: A pilot evaluation."* International Journal of Therapy & Rehabilitation (13)5 223-228

6) *Glasgow Coma Scale* May 9 2003. CDC: Department of Health and Human Services, Centers for Disease Control and Prevention. Retrieved on January 22, 2014 from www.bt.cdc.gov/masscasualties

7) Gurreridge, Debroah, MS, CBIS, Kansas City, MO. April 4, 2013. *"Different Faces of Brain Injury: Adjustment, Coping and Accepting."* 7th Annual Nebraska Brain Injury Conference. Younes Conference Center, Kearney, NE April 4 & 5, 2013, Lecture

8) Hayes, Ron PhD (Summer 2010) *"TBI in the US Military"* The Challenge: Page 5

9) Healy, M. November 20, 2013. *"Could a Blood Test Detect Concussions with Lasting Disability?"* Retrieved from Los Angeles Times at http://articles.latimes.com/2013/nov/20/science/la-sci-blood-test-concussion-20131119

10) Ishibe, N. ScD, Wlordarczyk R. BS., Fulco, C. MS. *"Overview of the institute of Medicine's Committee Search Strategy and Review Process for Gulf War and Health: Long-term Consequences of Traumatic Brain Injury."* Journal of Head Trauma Rehabilitation. Vol 24, No6 pp 434-429 2009 Wolters Kluwer Health, Lippincott Williams & Wilkins

11) Leibson CL, Brown AW, Long KH, Ransom JE, Mandrekar J, Osler TM, Malec MF: ." July 20, 2012 *"Medical Care Costs Associated with Traumatic Brain Injury over the Full Spectrum of Disease: A Controlled Population-Based Study."* July 20, 2012 Journal of Neurotrauma, 29: 2038-2049

12) 'Living with Brain Injury: The Consequences of Brain Injury." Page 2 Brain Injury Association of Nebraska. Retrieved on November 14, 2013 at www.biane.org/what/

13) McDonough, Victoria Tilner: " February 2010 : *"Vision Issues After Brain Injury: BrainLine talks with Dr. Gregory Goodrich.* Retrieved on March 28, 2010 from www.brainline.org/content/2010/02/vision-issues-after-brain-injury-brainline-talks-with-Dr-Gregory-Goodrich

14) McIlvanie, Rob.(June 6, 2012) "Trials for Traumatic Brain Injury blood test underway." The United States Army. Retrieved January 10, 2014 from www.army.mil/article/81204/Trials_for_traumatic_brain_injury_blood_test_underway

15) McMillian T M, Jongen, E L M M, Greenwood RJ. (1996) *"Assessment of post-traumatic amnesia after severe closed head injury: retrospective or prospective*? Journal of Neurology, Neurosurgery, and Psychiatry. Pages 422-427

16) *"Motor Vehicle Safety."* Page 1. CDC Center for Disease Control and Prevention: Retrieved on November 15, 2013 from www.cdc.gov/motorvehiclesafety

17) *"Nebraska Statistics: Nebraska TBI Needs and Resources Assessment Survey."* Page 1 Brain Injury Association of Nebraska. Retrieved on November 14, 2013 at www.biane.org/what/nebraska.html

18) *"Nebraska TBI needs and Resources Assessment Survey."* Page 1. Retrieved on November 14, 2013 from www.biane.org/what/nebraska.html

19) Olson, Eric. :University of Nebraska's new CB3 Research Center Will Study Concussions. July 4.2013, Retrieved on February 3, 2014,from www.huffingtonpost.com/2013/07/05/university-of-nebraska-concussions-cb3-research.

20) "Oregon Concussion Awareness and Management Program (OCAMP), Straight Talk about Concussion: It's a Brain Injury. It's serious." Retrieved January 20, 2014 from www.Brain101.orcasinc.com

21) *"Resources for People with Brain Injury and Their Families."* TBI National Resource Center, Virginia Commonwealth University, Neuropsychology and Rehabilitations Psychology Division, Department of Physical Medicine and Rehabilitation, Retrieved on January 9, 2014 from www.tbirc.com/resources-for-people-with-brain-injury-and-their-families.

22) *"Returning to Work after TBI."* September, 2007 Rainbow Visions Magazine, Rainbow Rehabilitation Centers, 5570 Whittaker Road, Ypsilanti, MI 48197. Page 1-4

23) Rusty McKune MS, ATC. University of Nebraska Sports Medicine Program Coordinator. "Return to Learn: Bridging the Gap between Concussion and the Classroom." 7th Annual Nebraska Brain Injury Conference. Younes Conference Center, Kearney, Nebraska April 4 & 5, 2013. Lecture

24) Shively, S, MD, PhD, Perl, D, MD *"Traumatic Brain Injury, Shell Shock, and Posttraumatic Stress Disorder in the Military--Past, Present, and Future."* J Head Trauma Rehibilitation. Vol 27, No 3 // 234-239. 2012. Wolters Kluwer Health, Lippincott Williams & Wilkins.

25) "Signs and Symptoms of a Concussion." Brain Injury Association of Nebraska. Retrieved on November 7, 2013 from www.biane.org/sports/concussionsymptoms.html

26) Ruggeri R, Smedile G., Granata F., Longo M,. Cannavo S., Sarlis NJ., Trimarchi, F., Benvenga S. *"Spontaneous recovery from isolated post-traumatic central hypogonadism in a women."* Hormones, 2010 9(4) 332-337

27) The Human Brain, Wikipedia. The Free Encyclopedia Retrieved March 25, 2014 from http://en.wikipedia.org/wiki/Human_Brain

28) Tomaszewski, W., Manko, Grzegorz *"An evaluation of the strategic approach to the rehabilitation of traumatic brain injury (TBI) patients."* www.MedSciMoni.com 201: 17(9) CR510-516.

29) *"Traumatic Brain Injury"* Family Information Booklet 2nd Edition, Madonna Rehabilitation Hospital 5401 South Street, Lincoln, NE 68506

30) *"Treatment Centers."* 2013 TBI Treatment Centers: Retrieved on November 2013 from www.traumaticbraininjury.com/Injury-resources/treatment-center/, Pages 1&2

31) Weiner, W J, Porter N, Shin R, Lewis S L. (2010) Neurology for the Non-neurologist: Philadelphia, PA; Lippincott; Page 335

32) *"2010 Nebraska Traumatic Brain Injury: Needs and Resources* Assessment" Page 12 Retrieved on November 14, 2013 from www.braininjury.ne.gov/docs/10TBIassessment-ExecSum.pdf